Still Shall a Calling Hear Bell

Katie Parry // art

Heather Woods // poetry

Spuyten Duyvil
New York City

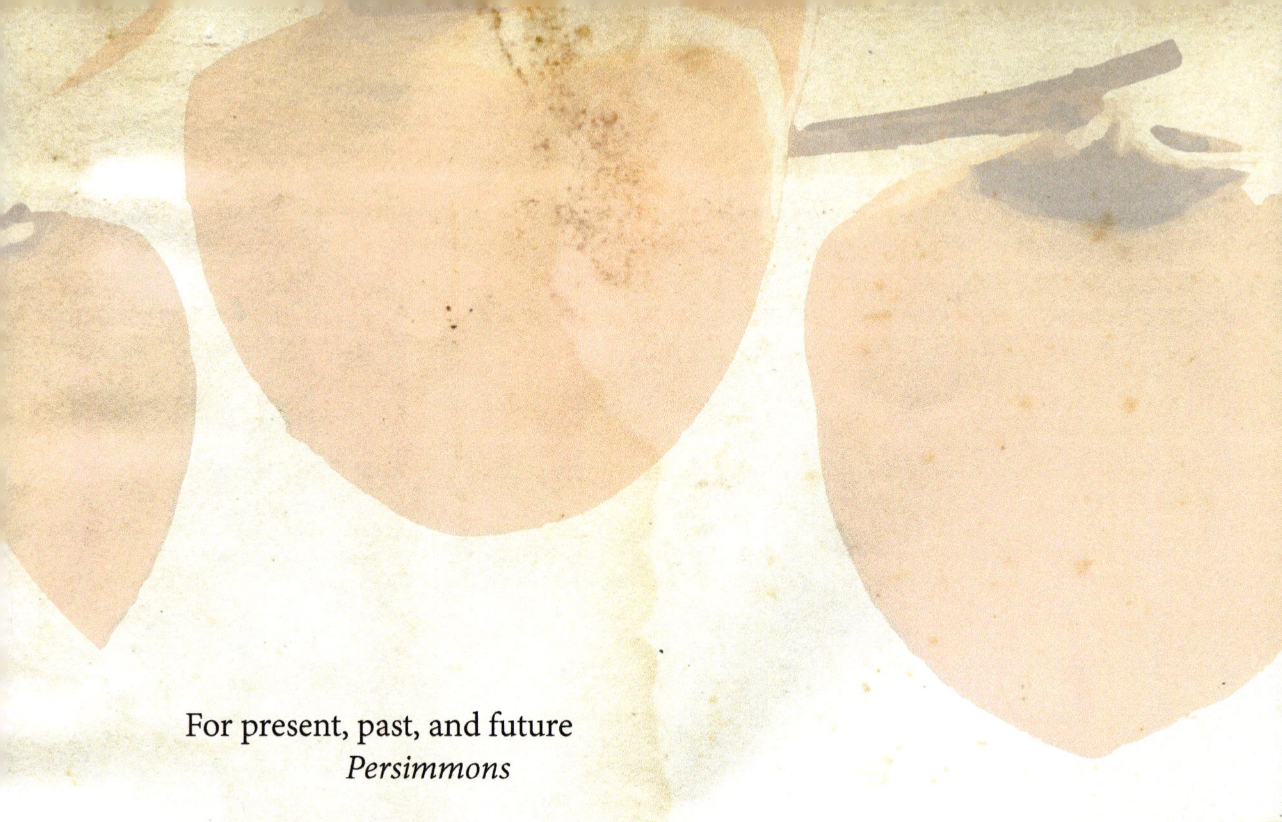

For present, past, and future
Persimmons

The roots
  below the earth
    claim no rewards
  for making the branches
    fruitful.

Rabindranath Tagore, *Stray Birds*

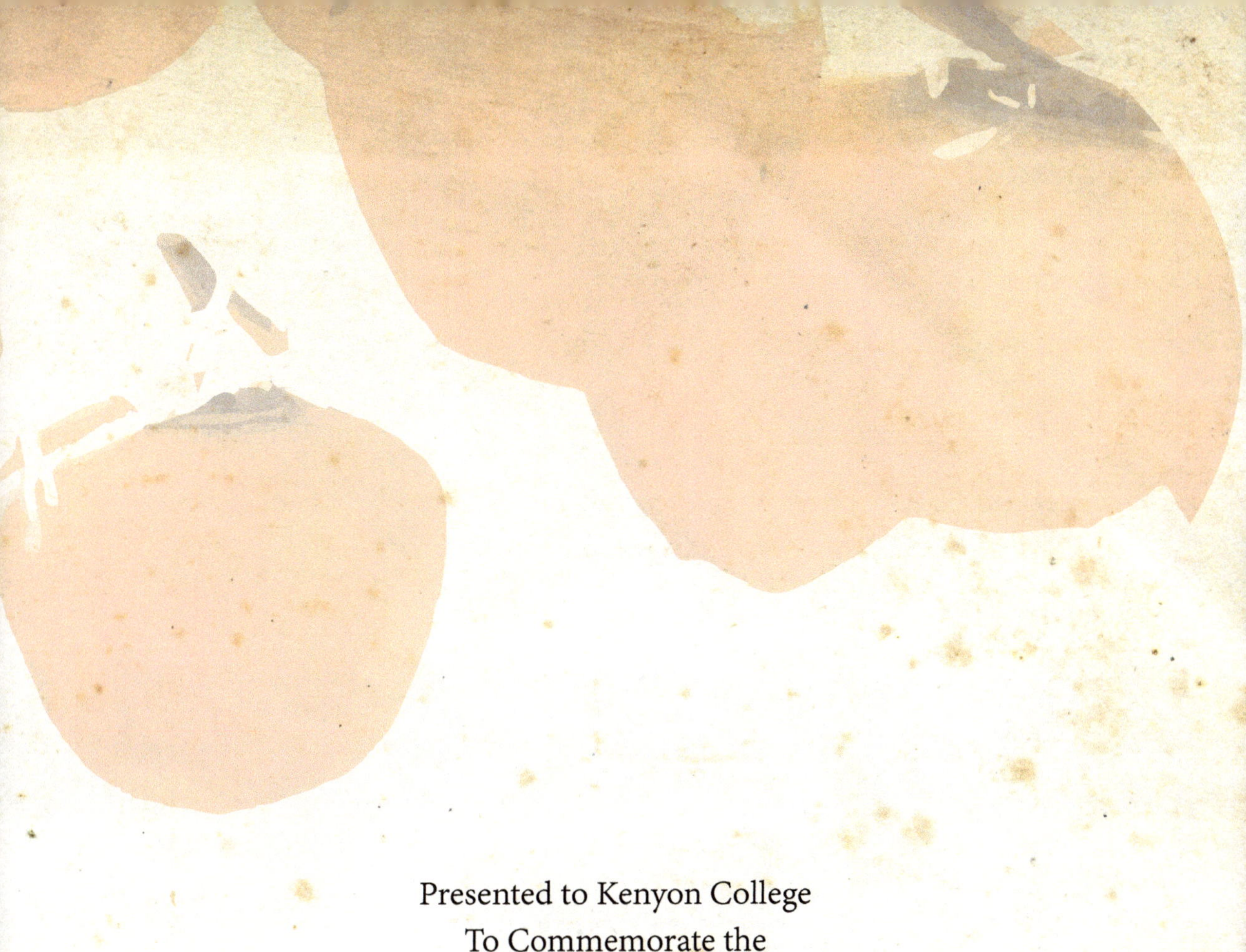

Presented to Kenyon College
To Commemorate the
25th Anniversary Celebration
of *Persimmons Literary Magazine*
2021-2022

There exists no phenomena except what exists in the mind.
Other than fruition that occurs, where is the one who is realizing the fruit?

~ Padmasambhava's terma
"Self-Liberation Through Seeing with Naked Awareness"

Oh, the feel of the wolftail on the silk,
the strength, the tense
precision in the wrist.
I painted them hundreds of times
eyes closed. These I painted blind.
Some things never leave a person:
scent of the hair of one you love,
the texture of persimmons,
in your palm, the ripe weight.

~ Li-Young Lee
"Persimmons"

Be the student of everyone.

~ Shantideva
The Way of the Bodhisattva

Drink in the words like nectar
and be completely concentrated.
That is the way to listen to the teaching.

~ Patrul Rinpoche
Words of My Perfect Teacher

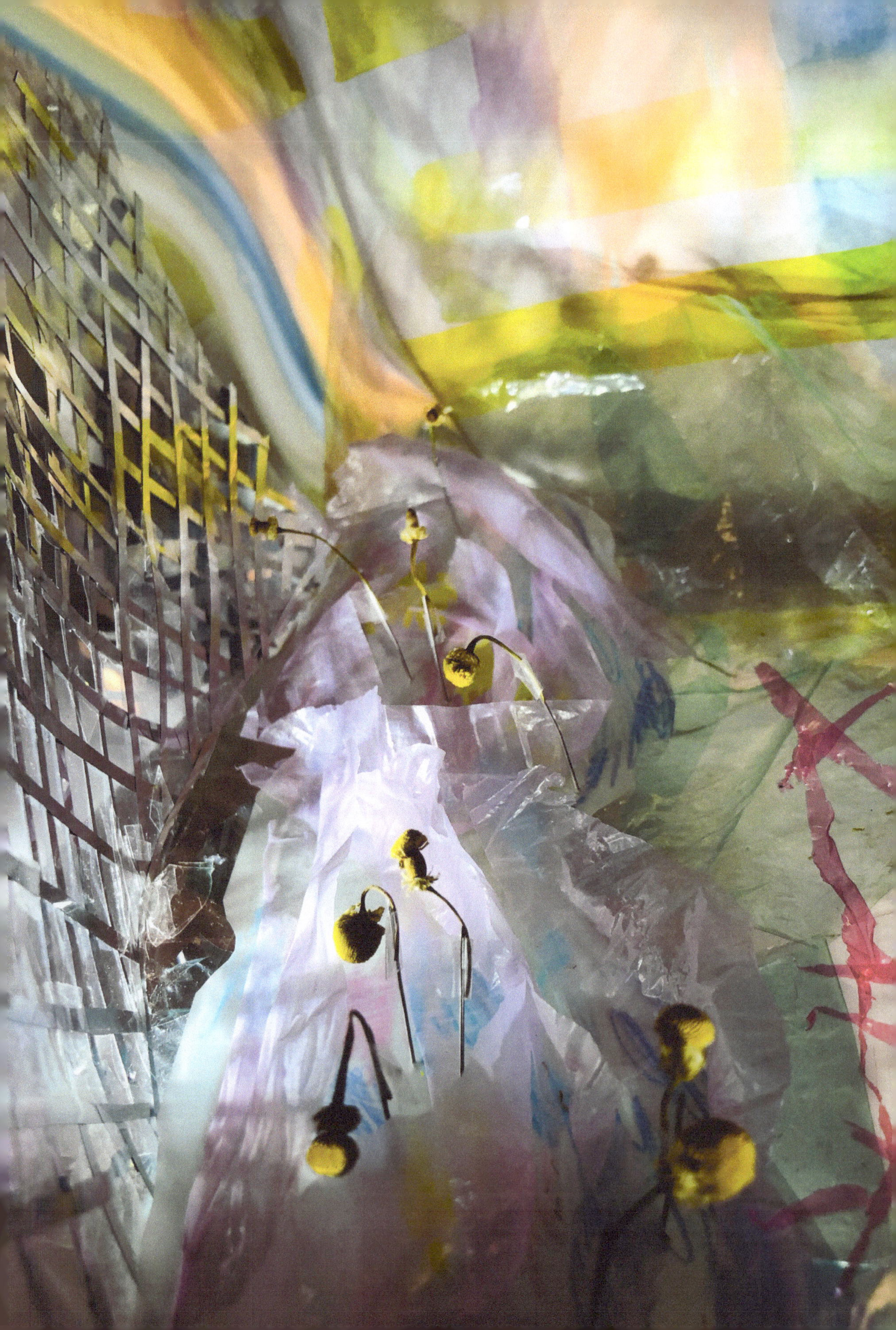

What conditions

have planted   me here
              ripening

to a sweet meat
                    sweetly meeting
                                        karmamudrā consort

the field   fecund floral   unfurls   able to absorb
                                                    the teachings

root system frayed   desiccated landscape

    crosses country   with humid brays

    self-seeding   for-Rest

afflictive arrogance of

    Degenerative Age   Regenerative Stage

    Persimmon Meader

must have a consort   present   to create fruit

Interdependent
                        Arising

                              grows best in cold climes

           Himalaya

                    where your teacher

                              played with old bones and sticks

              incantatory

     insects dancing their spirit show

  Fled to
                              preserve the sacred nectar of

  teachings
                              Drepung Loseling

  bury the terma   in the cave

              of your

                              where treaders can't reach

                    whilst I up on the hill

        studied the language of the oppressor

                Oh press her

        Yeshe Tsogyal /
                \Against a great wall

                                contre le mur

                                        une bouche crie

                escapes to Sky Azurey

                compass   passion
                        action
physical
                                        cyclical

                for the fruit to ripen

                do not pick when green

                when a gentle tug does not

                release

Sweet milk
of her orbs across the ages

Mater nubile
crisp pointed

Mater supple
nourishing
oozing

Mater shriveling

Mater puckering

Mater rotting

with one foot extended

and one tucked under

Persimmon crooked teat

not cute or built to suit

a fashionable mouth-meet

a woman in a doorway

seek refuge in

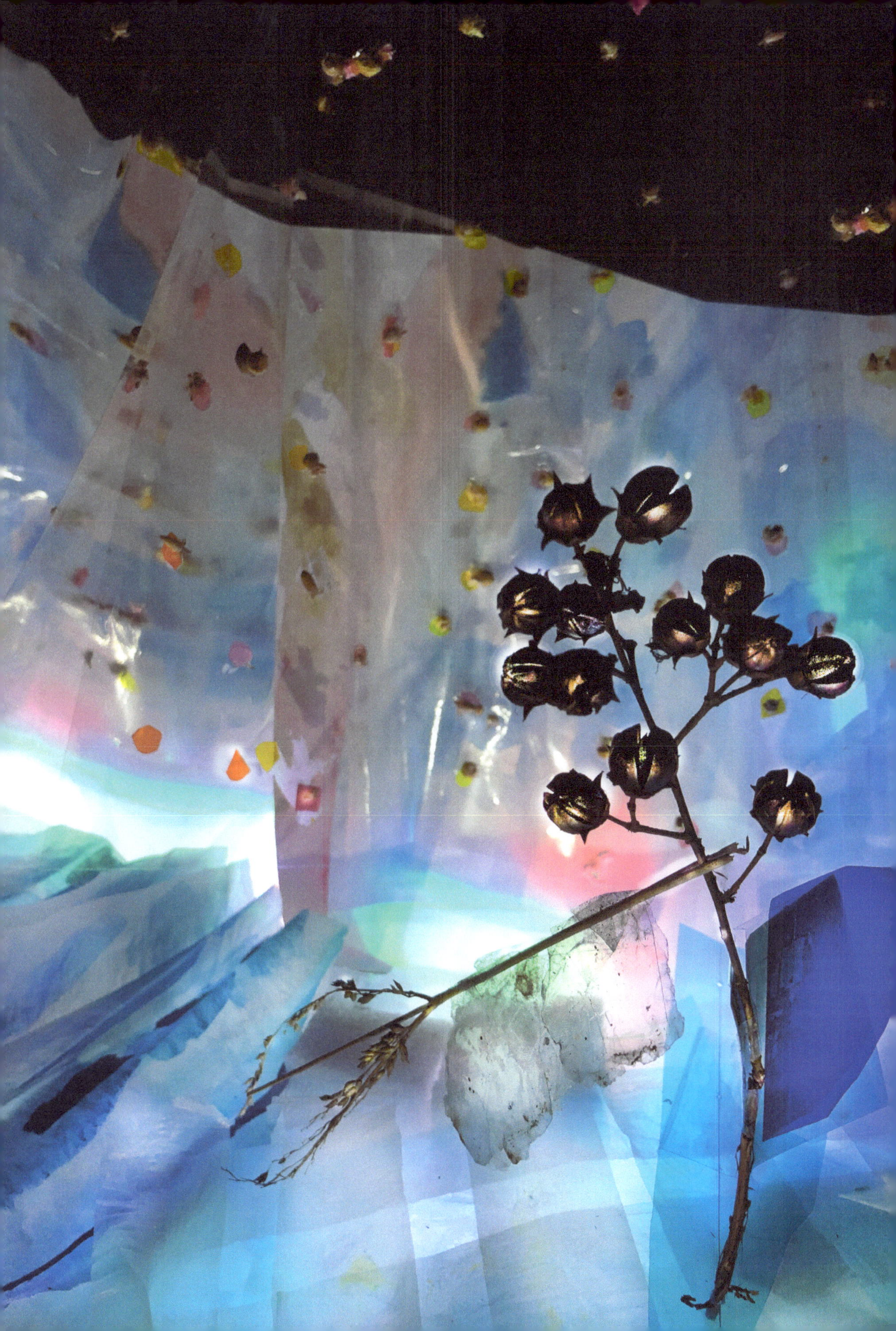

a mandala of sand
brightly hued
rainbow bodied
painstakingly placed
then blow

into Kokosing

mantra haunts   *poetry is prayer*

across the valley of the

Three times

              Victorious Bliss Gone Ones

meet in my mouth

bats at dusk   soaring out

              Norton

              Anthology of

Contempt   or Airy

statue of an

ecstatic embrace

     bare trees swallow up

        the sun

'more love and knowledge of you'

Yab-yum

masking the sweetness
with your soon to be bare
gums

Seek the middle
       way
        along Middle Path

touch the adamantine
erection

for luck   *or some kind of persimmon-jump*

        offer up
        torso to the
        Buddha field

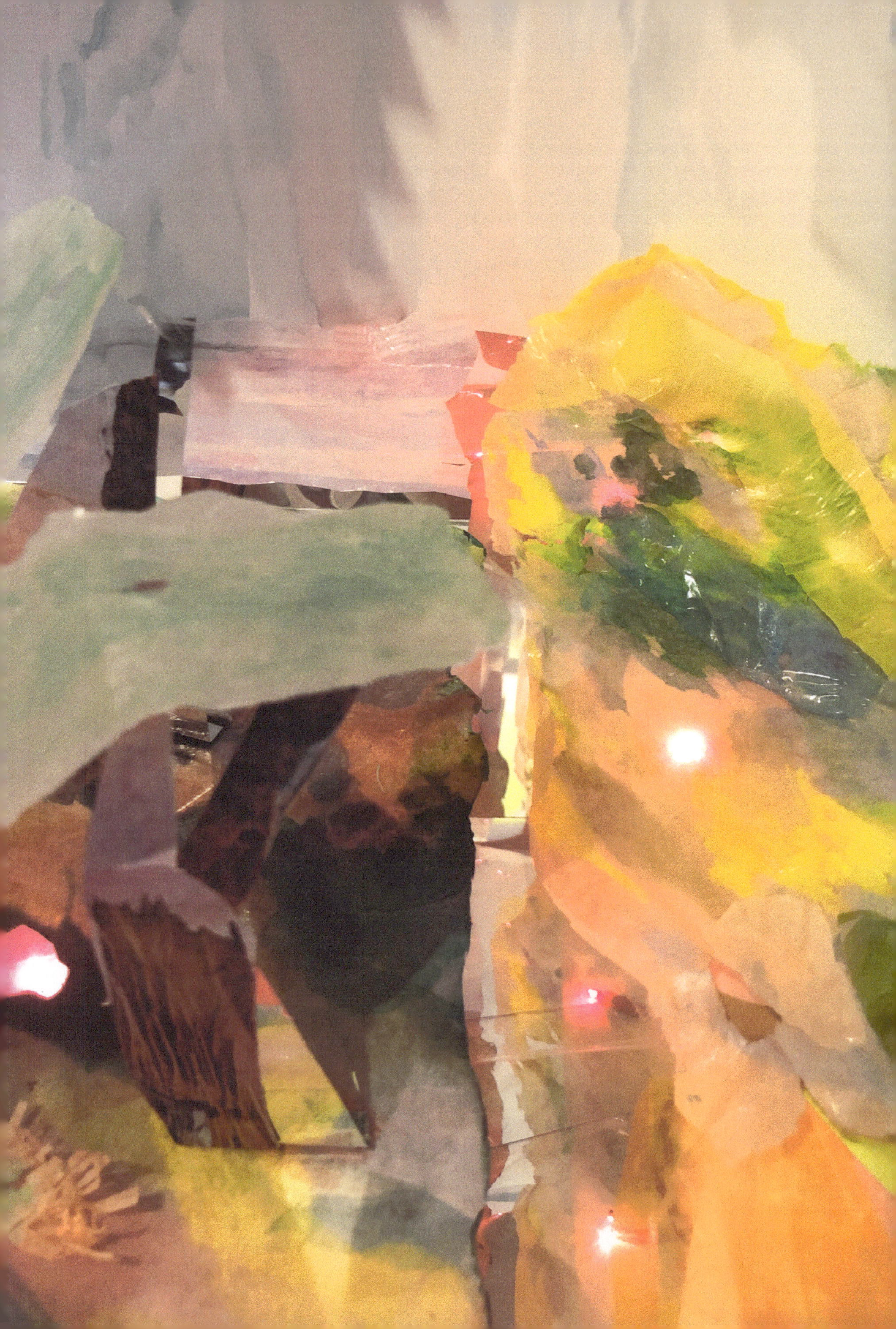

treading
equanimity

I'm not special
Being

Human   translate a rare
                                                  character

                          Jack starts
                          every lesson
                          with green tea and
                          dark chocolate
                          repleting every nerve
                          to impart

Just like you

                    balancing orange globes

                              Her stumble on All of These Things

                    apply the antidote

            still the walls do not fall

lifetime after lifetime

karmic fruit ripens

what connections have I made

no grafting needed   Quarter Century
the seeds planted
shoot far
fruit
                How tall you are
                                our starry shoot

  'Deep tawnie cullour'   *of sunset*
Each orb some light   *left from summer*
Glowing on brown   *fall ground*
the persimmons
are flowing
                chasing down
                        SUNYATA
            unknowing it
                already In

which beareth naught upon its swell

                                        Emptiness
        the Womb
                    of Compassion

Her hands trace me   *Traçant des halos sur les mers*
            calligraph of

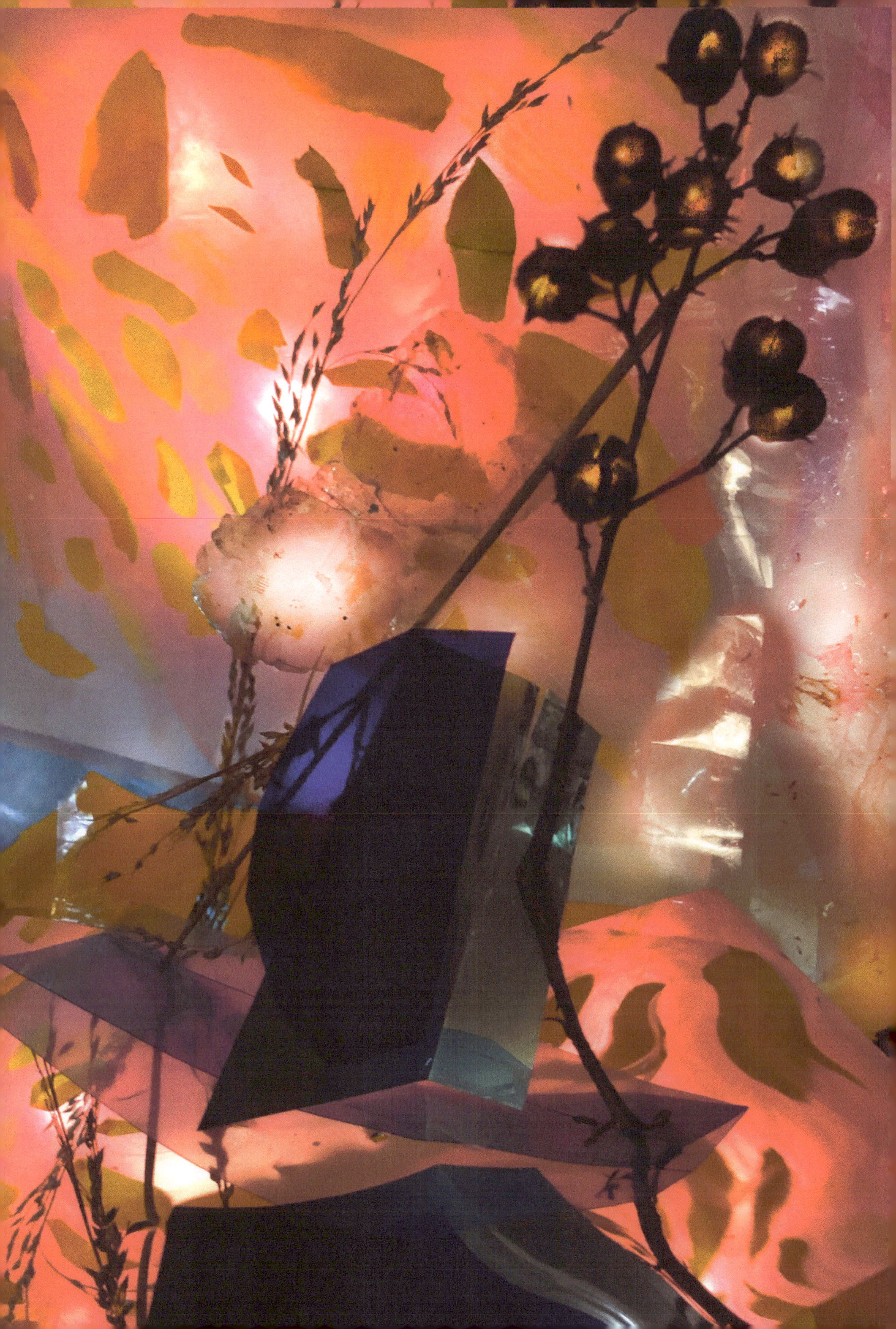

a line replete

magnetic essence stand

still shall hear a calling bell

if you are fully present for

SEM
would not have attained
RIGPA
Had she not fed him

Kheer
milk sweet of her

tear through the skin that

coagulates on the surface

with cashews
with rose petals
with saffron

cardamom

the need for my care

love's labors
scrub
else milk

scorch flare

How could he knot   Attain

                    mullioned
            Mind-stream

                        I begin to believe the only sin is distance

                            gargoyles
                    mount   Sheela na gigs

            Mound builders   flout abstention

bearing the burnt
            Amber moon   mist mussed music

                    a cantering buggy

                        foretells
            bearded bonnets
                    stone ground loaves

                        Holy rollers over

'pessamin'
                        a dry fruit

Powhatan

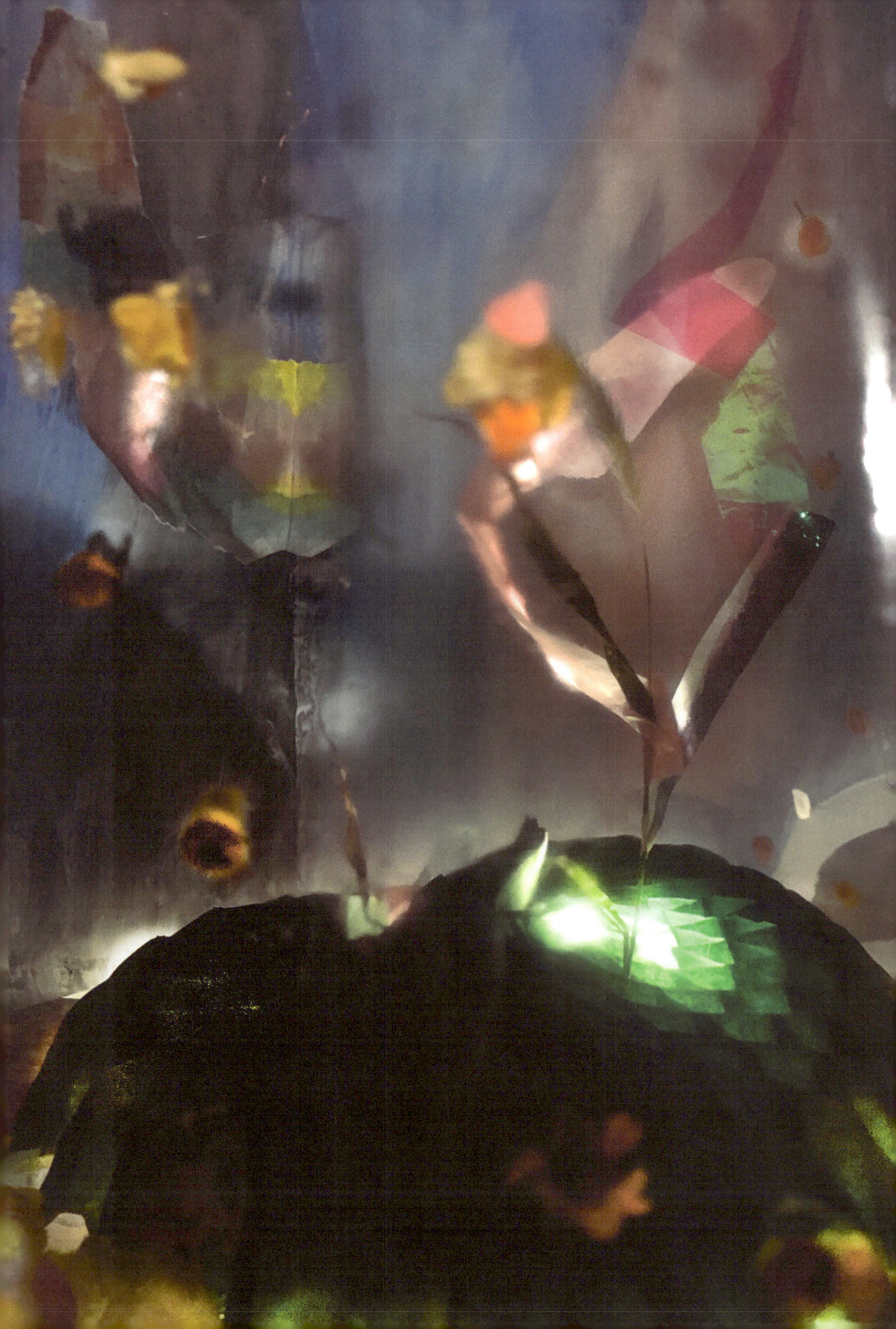

Whose spirits
carry our   *the ripe weight*
dwelling
here on this land

even briefly   memoir in
                                your hand

        urges us from all reposing

                                feel its skin
                                        shiver
                                shimmer
                                        slime
                                sublime

        grows best in peat free soil

                loam and loess

                nutrient rich

                        matrilineal   matrilocal

                                woodland

        Ascension

                                        of pure being

                        What has been said to me,

                        how has my life replied?

going down to the underworld

her fanged incanting

    cantos   Bard-O

        Sing
to bind a fascicle

for a future to be
possible   Seeps I

         narrative in sepia

Marian Anderson
aria weeps
        each steep step
          eternal stamp
           mash your
           persimmon
         palimpsest

        iamb underfoot
      mandala of sound
     spondee sprung rhythm

   swift, slow; sweet, sour; adazzle, dim;

heard
       in the orchestral dark

Ophelia a last

pastoral gesture of love toward the world

When round us evening shades are closing

Beside our
hodgepodge
Pad Thai
one jar
brown butter
and some noodles
enough to sate
letters of longing

we say, because desire is full of
endless distances

We do not appear as
Couple ought
our commingling caught

too many flavors   the restaurant reserves the right
for a bland state   to unseat us

My bygone love   *Naked, I teach her*
Ni // Wo

 you were brave
to visit

from the fires

ravage redwoods

Gone, gone Beyond

to meadows sweet with asphodel

The moment I set foot I knew

where to plant my

Want a poem

I can grow old in

easting the west

California I'm coming   *Double Vie de*
Home   *Veronique*

heart skips

I'll even kiss that sunset   scattered across
pink   The Three Times

life full of suffering

also full of

days that are the good flesh continuing

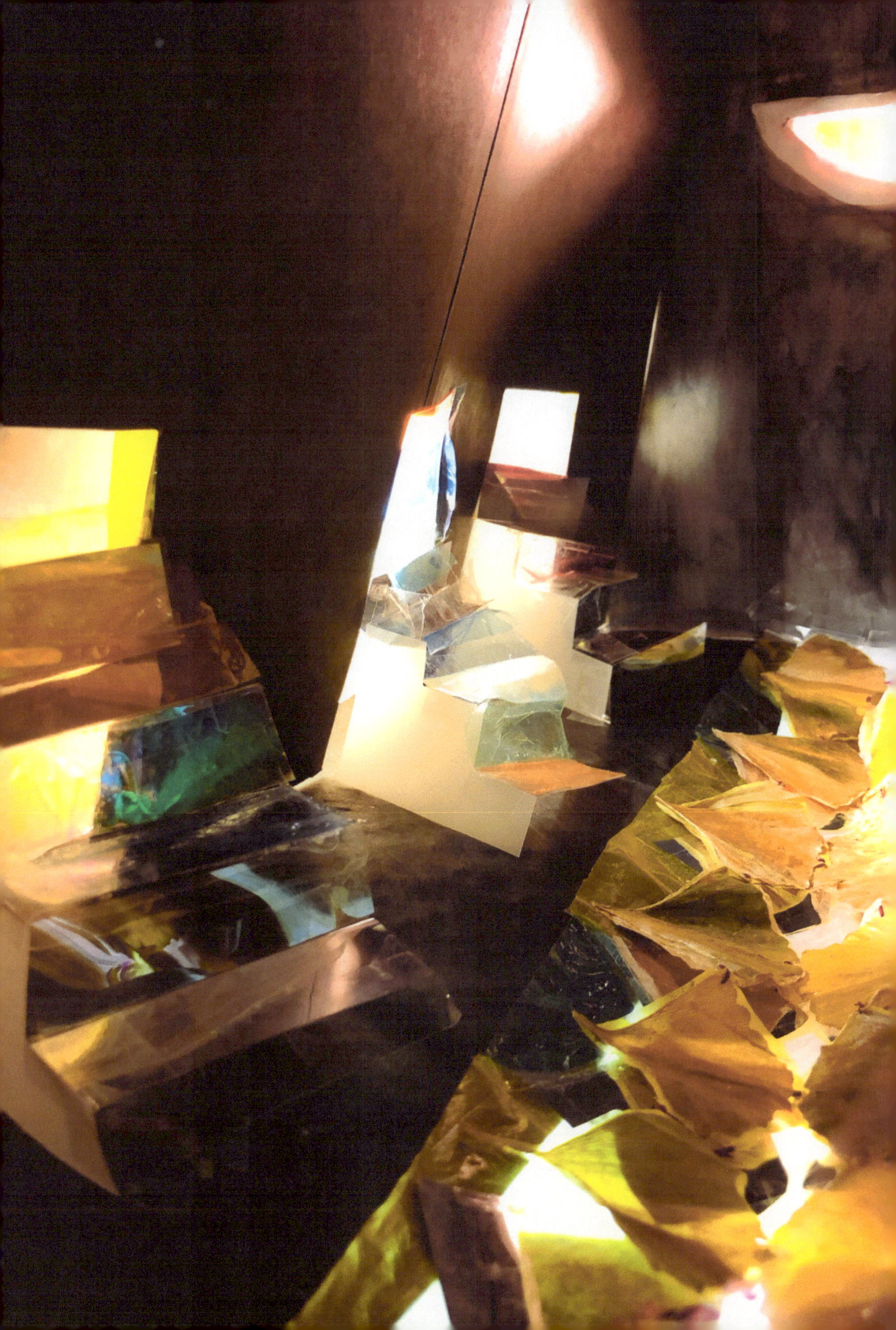

Persimmons

ripening in hand
            respond to the warmth of your

            immutable touch

            Moon stranger

sniff the bottoms   *the sweet one*

            will be fragrant

            tenderly tear

here dear

        bite into the ripples

        as you spread

ashes of our Quiet flower
            ring

Vienne la nuit
        sonne l'heure

            Les jours s'en vont
                je demeure

I demure
     You   persimmon tree
                  now forty plus
  feet tall

     Year upon year
                Skyey aspiring

the refugees

        of the library
          clove saffron robes flow
             Atrium aglow
Sky-lit heart   cavity

   precise preparation

ease tiny granules
         touch my inner mystery

to reveal our common divinity

       BODHICHITTA

  Seekers

We follow

  sound blowing down

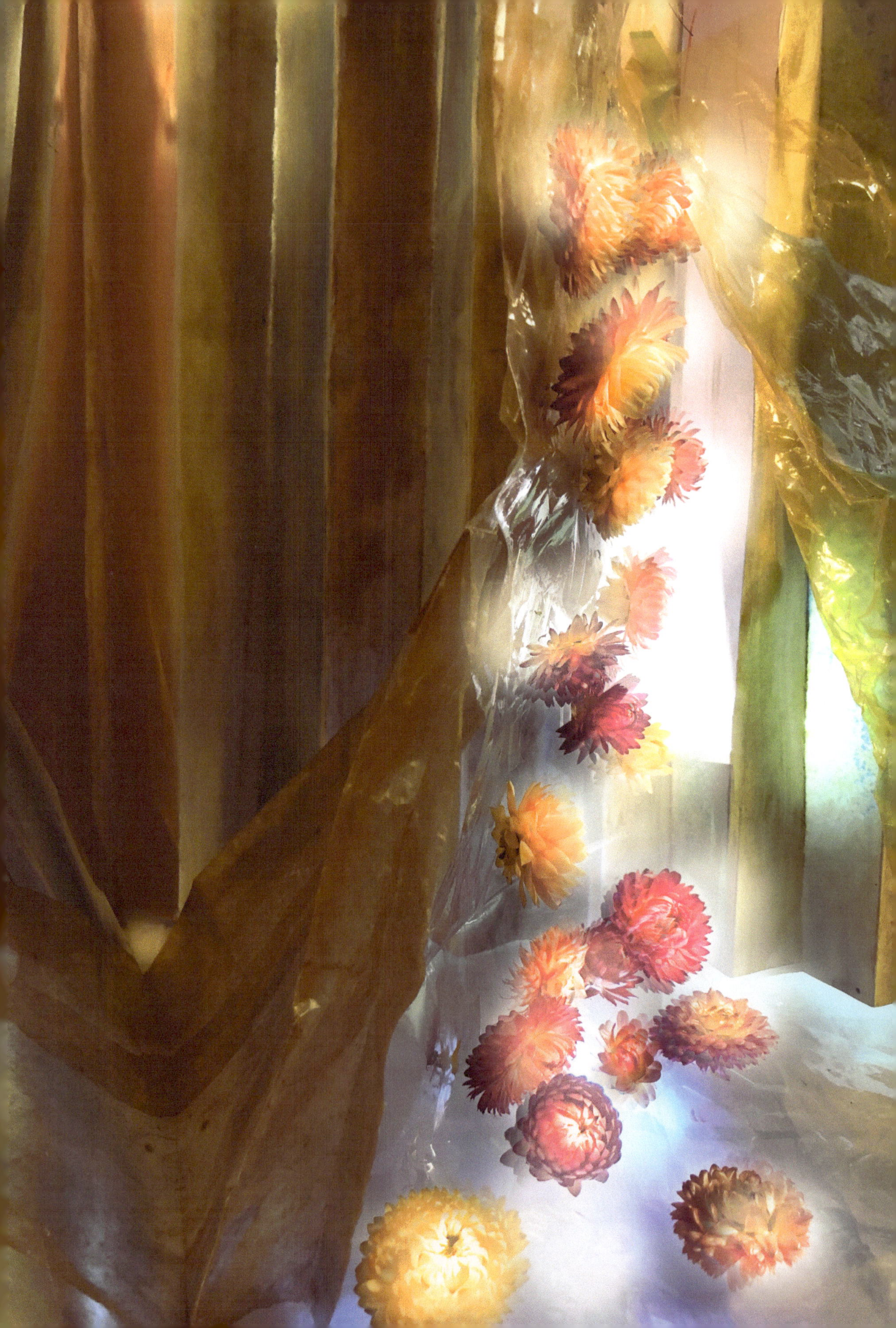

to the river rove

    that flows unceasingly

        Kokosing

   Come

  Rivers, come

       Allons

   Irrevocable futures

     come

Nos multiples horizons

          paddle heart

      let go let Go

    the eternal maker

  only the breath

 ceases

How bright the sand

   pour us river

  foam of motion's own composing

paddle lotus

Let go let go

into the water douse

the maker and her artifact

teardrop on fire

the days flow by me

still I stay

talking to a rainbow

round topped

misconceived

fruit in fact a berry

leaves leathery

glossy go brown silk slow

male flowers pink

females creamy

a perfect flower   houses both

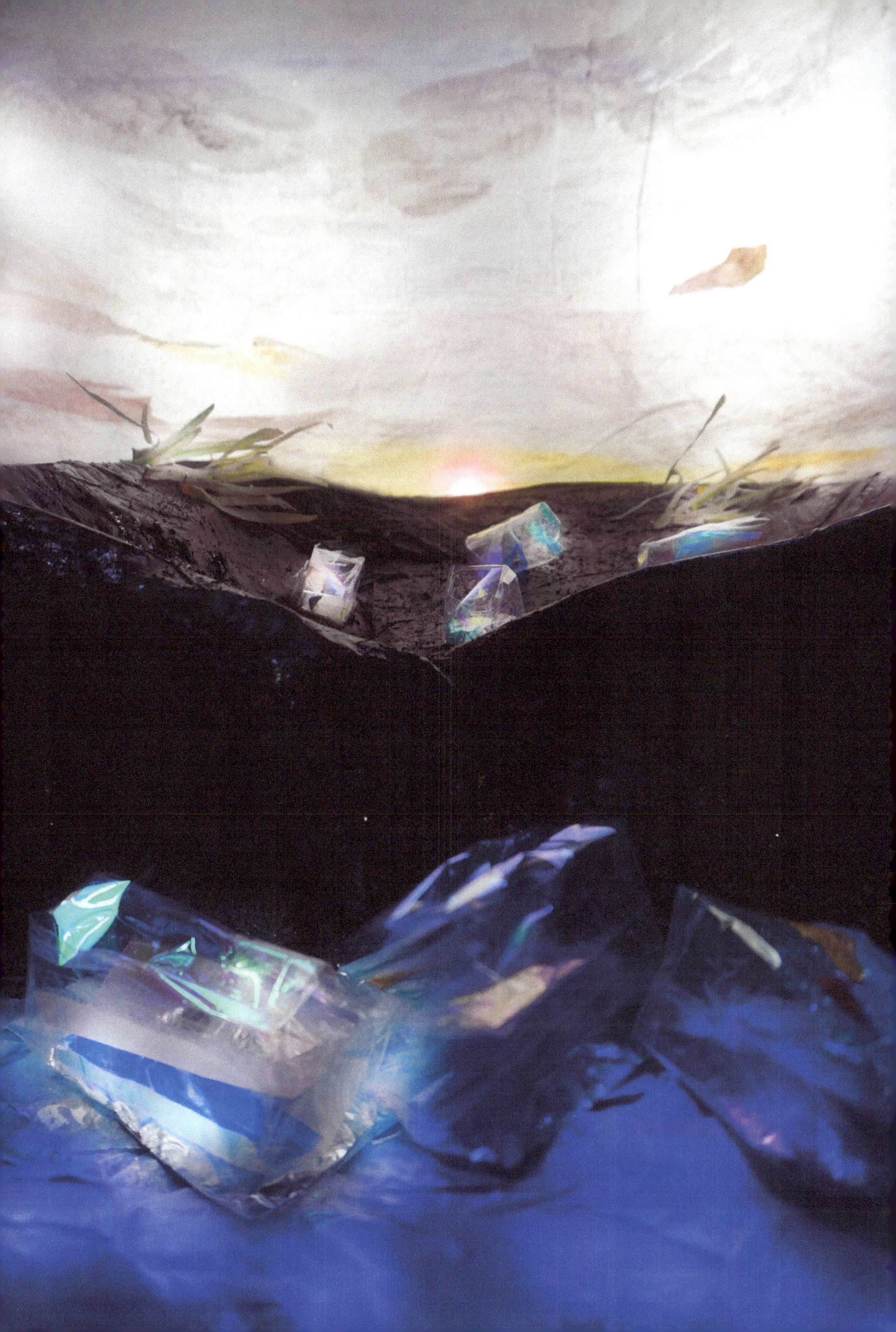

do not bite until ripe

full and emptied

bowls on the table

imagine airy persimmons

promises

on the altar

you place for

those Gone

Gone Beyond

PARINIRVANA

His head is gold
as he enters
her center
rainbow colored

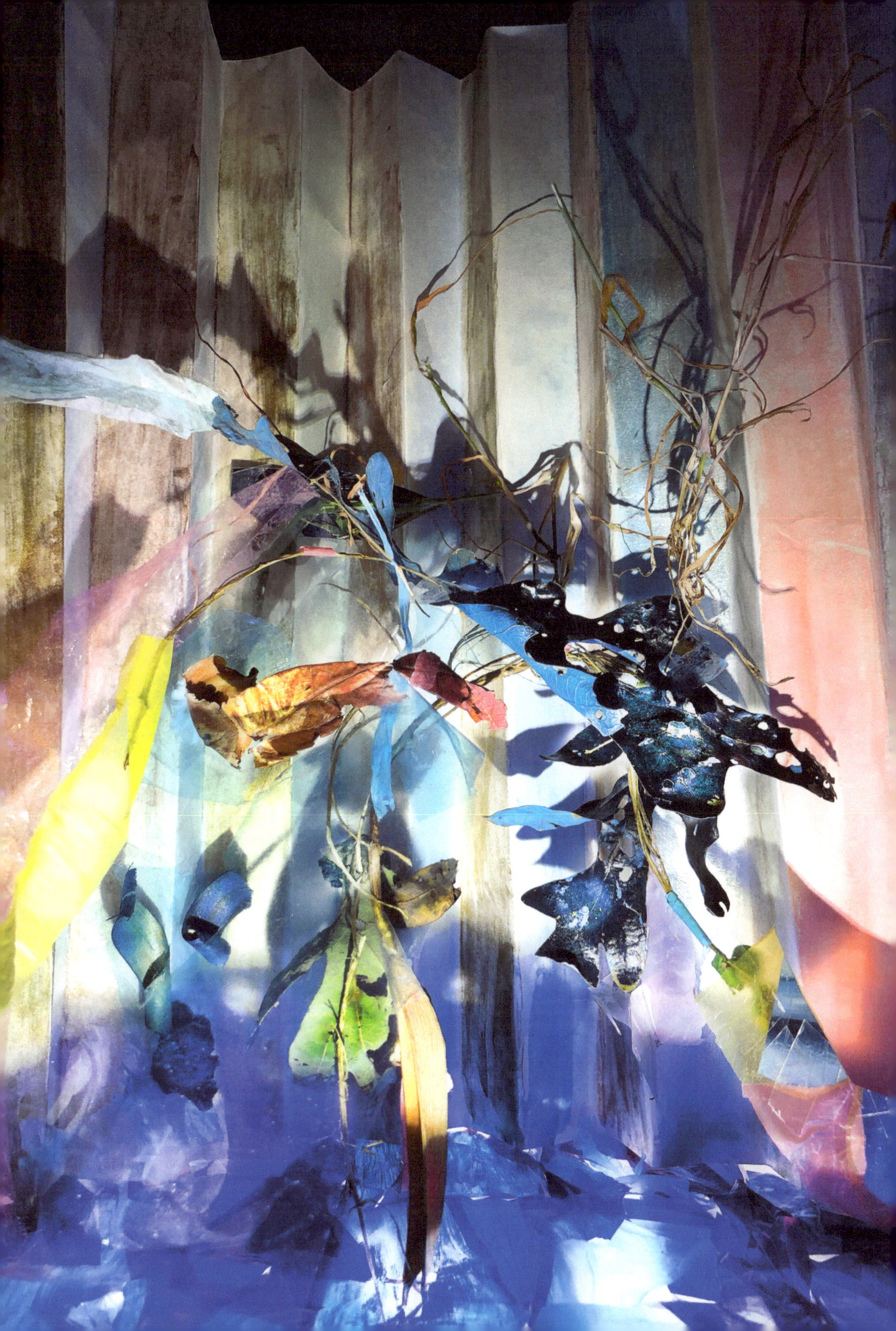

I ride   *I ride*

dancing onto the   *tongue of heaven*

Who wants for nothing

yet feels a deep need

plant this Seed

         & persimmon ripens

             Just as I leave

Redolent night

    we mouth music

  our Inmost musk

       Mantra that draws forth

star-stuff

Words
say everything

Bite down

feel the pressure

a round within a round

'gracefully nervous'

take care to chew

you want so much so little

Then what are words for

what
is emptiness
for

to fill
fill

I heard words   full
of holes
aching

speech is a

moth   budding

twilit flame

                                        soft spotted

        tender treader

                Who else

                                Where mem'ry

mammary

                sweet nectar render

                                        cello suites

                        dangling chord   besotted

                dwells dear

        past supposing   hollow closing

                        faerie glow

        can stay on the tree through

                                winter

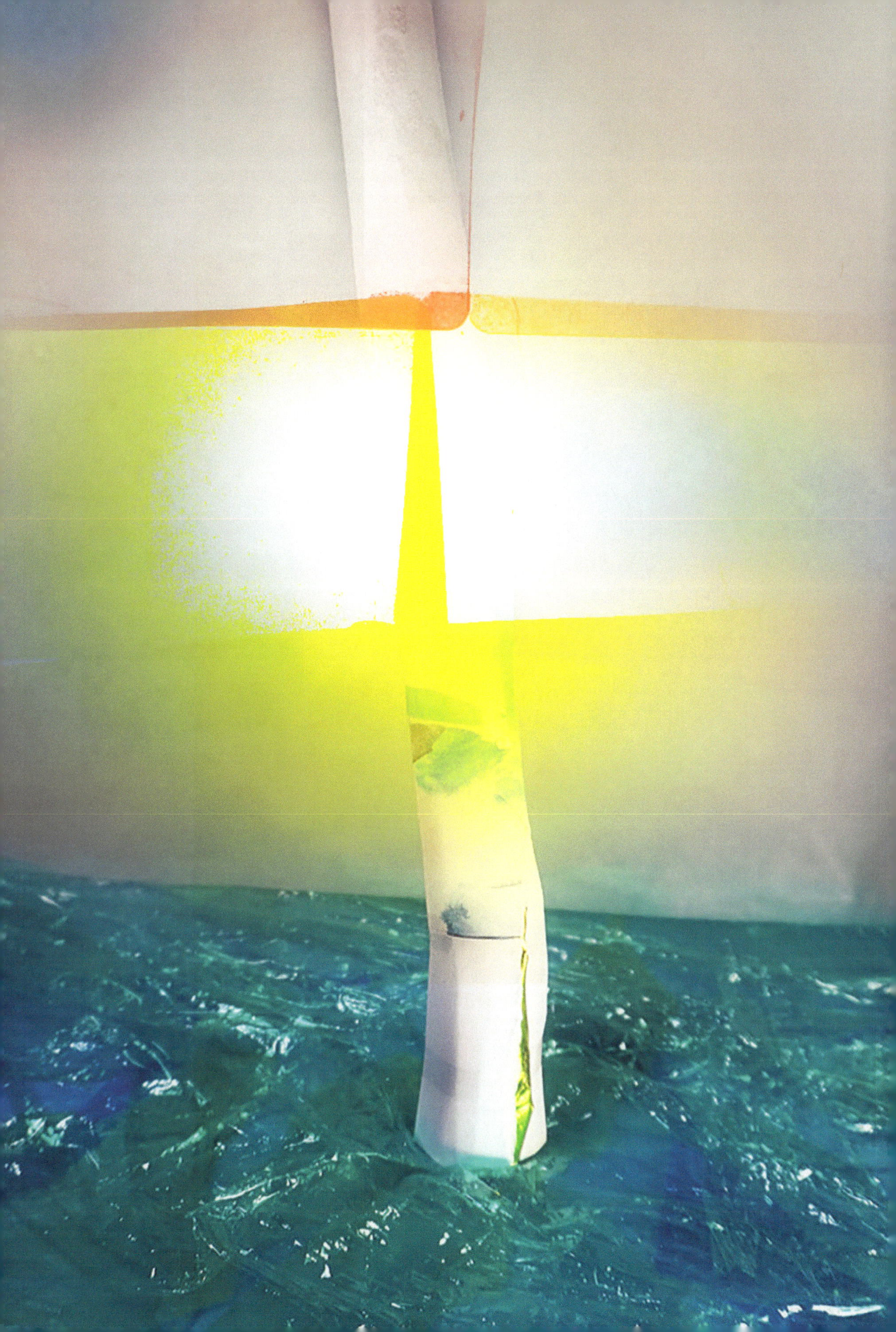

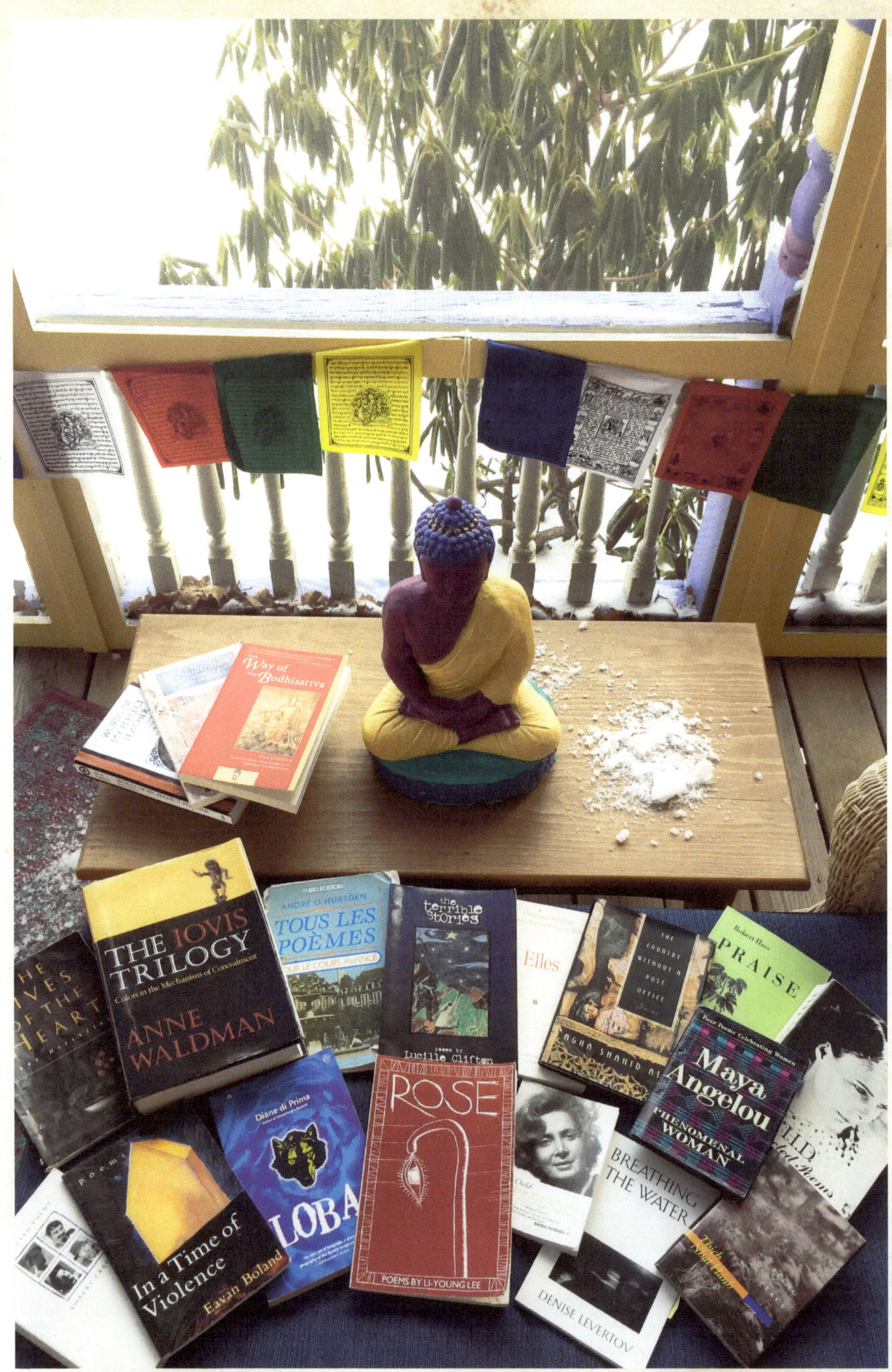

Still Shall Hear
    a Calling Bell
        Italics, in order of appearance

Amina Saïd, *Elles*, "comme un arbre"

Maya Angelou, *Phenomenal Woman*

Eavan Boland, *In a Time of Violence*

"Kokosing Farewell"

Samuel Beckett, *Disjecta: Miscellaneous Writings and a Dramatic Fragment*

Professor Rogan, Graduation Speech, to class of '99

Allen Ginsberg speaking on Anne Waldman

Anne Waldman, *Iovis*

H.D., *Trilogy*

Gary Snyder, *Left Out in the Rain*, "Persimmons"

Andrée Chedid, "Homme parmi les pierres"; "La vérité"

Jane Hirshfield, *The Lives of the Heart*, "Salt Heart"

Li-Young Lee, *Rose*, "Persimmons"

Denise Levertov, *Poems, 1968-1972*, "The Rain"

Robert Duncan, *The Years as Catches: First Poems*, 1939-1946, "An African Elegy"

Gerard Manley Hopkins, "Pied Beauty"

Robert Hass, *Praise*, "Meditation at Lagunitas"

Joni Mitchell, *Blue*, "California"

Krzysztof Kieślowski, *La Double Vie de Veronique*

Thich Nhat Hanh, *Being Peace*

Guillaume Apollinaire, "Le Pont Mirabeau"

Agha Shahid Ali, *The Country Without a Post Office*, "Farewell"

Massive Attack, "Teardrop"

Lucille Clifton, *the terrible stories*, "hag riding"; "what manner of man"

Diane di Prima, *Loba*

Robert Creeley, *Words*, "The Language"

Yo-Yo Ma, J.S. Bach, *The 6 Unaccompanied Cello Suites Complete*

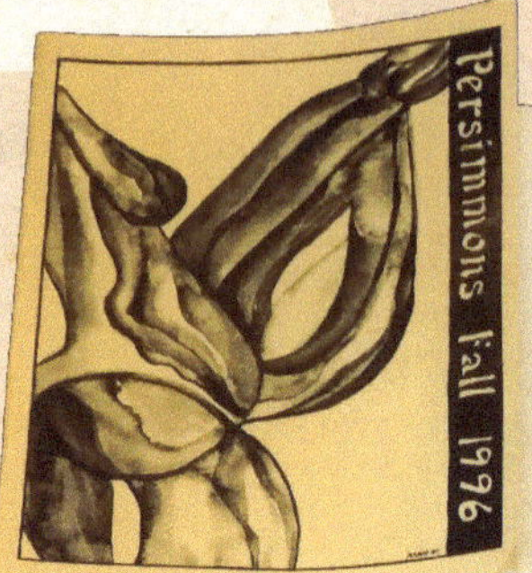

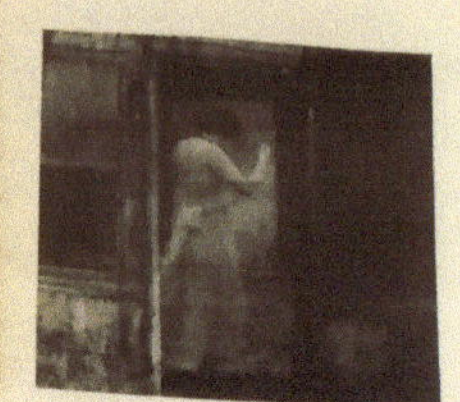

Persimmons

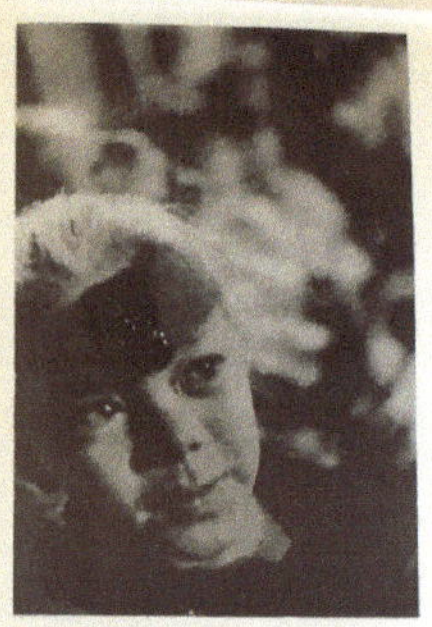

PERSIMMONS

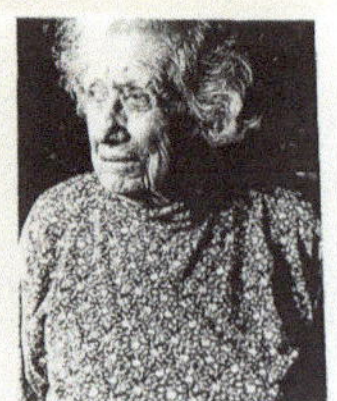

Persimmons.

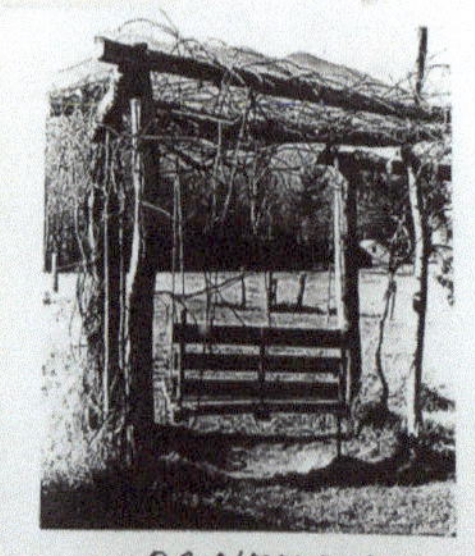

persimmons

*Still Shall Hear
a Calling Bell*

Reverberant Conversation
with
Katie Parry & Heather Woods

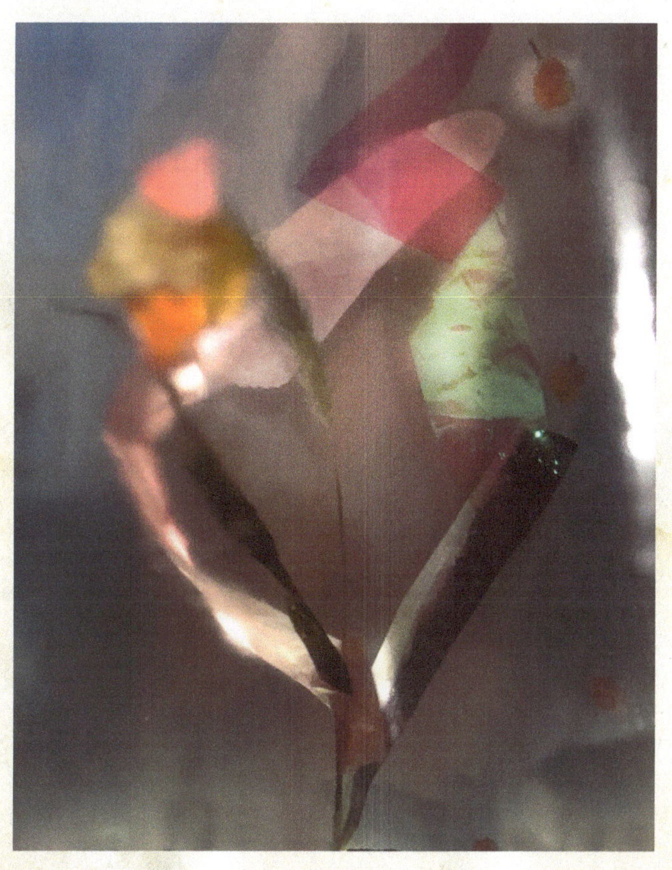

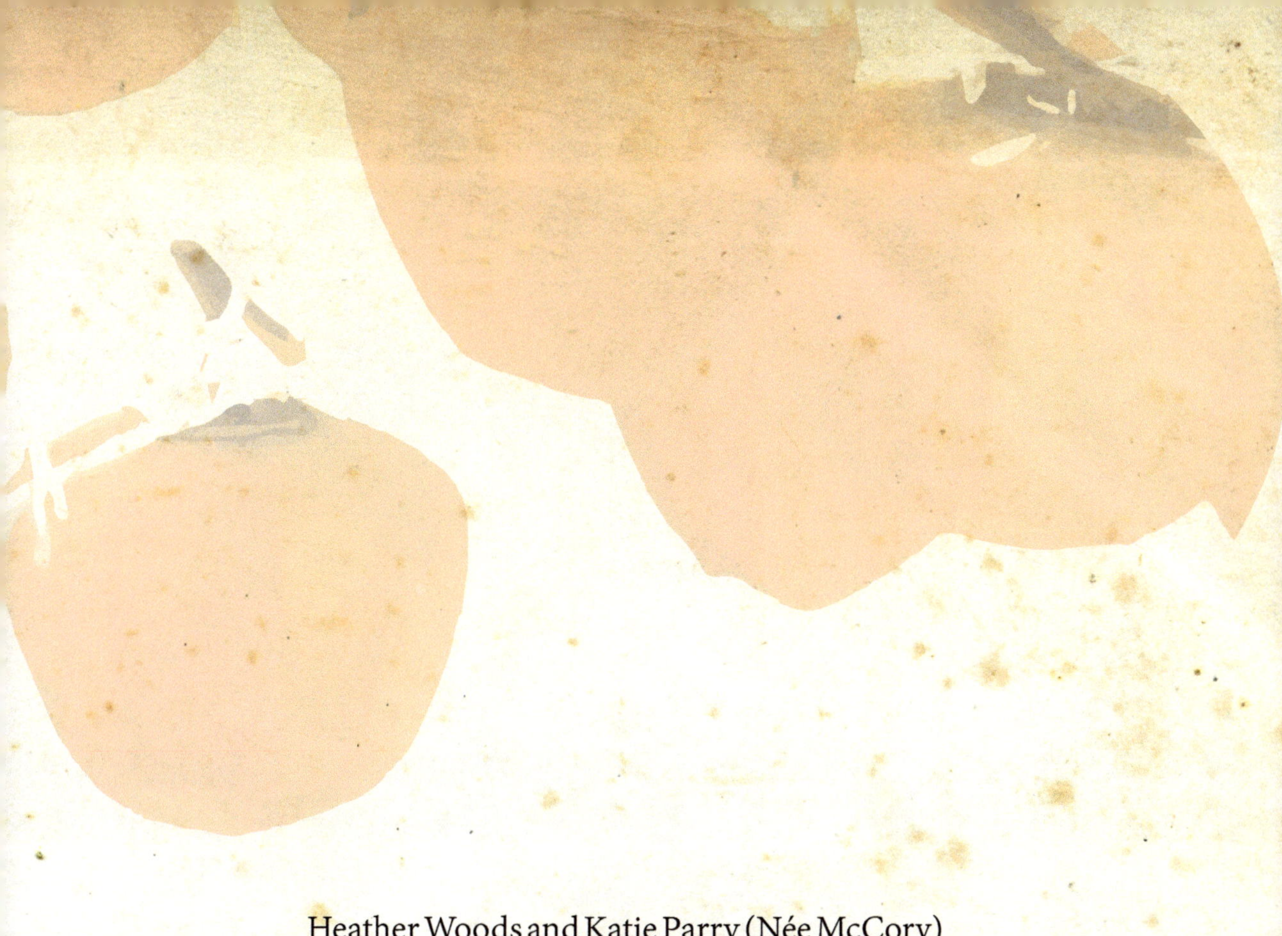

Heather Woods and Katie Parry (Née McCory) co-founded *Persimmons* literary magazine at Kenyon College, in autumn of 1996, after rooming together their freshman year. Kenyon generously supported the printing of *Persimmons* through yearly grants.

Why create *Persimmons?*

HW: We aspired to offer a more expansive forum for writers and artists on campus—we sensed there was a fecund field of gifted creators just waiting to unfurl. We generated a steady stream of encouraging email blasts re submissions and posted flyers and artful submission boxes all over campus; we sought to inspire varied voices across campus to offer their art for consideration by a supportive community. We really relished each submission and viewed each offering as just that—a gift, worthy of deep consideration. We also wanted to create a convivial communal selection process fostering democratic discernment. How satiating to know current editors have continued with this spacious tradition!

In our day, *Persimmons* was printed and bound by the Kenyon College Print Shop in Gambier—we started out with grainy prints but over time they skillfully refined our photos and art to be crisper, more defined. Before coming to Kenyon, I learned layout from four high school years of editing and managing a literary journal—we used Pagemaker (an early version of InDesign) back then. At Kenyon, I remember myriad late layout nights in the basement of (I believe) Ascension Hall, where the computer lab held its own electromagnetic rush.

We held most meetings in the Crozier Memorial Center for Women, and we held our readings on the KC stage at the Red Door Cafe (Wiggin St Coffee now). One of our favorite aspects of *Persimmons* was holding colorful readings—we especially enjoyed mixing media—we incorporated art, music and even a hint of modern dance into the readings as well as inviting audience participation by writing a collaborative poem during the event. We also made sure to offer plenty of delectable treats and fresh flowers to delight the senses. We remember *Persimmons* readings were quite densely packed—truly a sublime time.

How was the current project, *Still Shall Hear/ a Calling Bell,* born?

HW:　We were contacted by Bruno Trindade, class of '99, and former editor of *Persimmons*, who had reached out to current *Persimmons* editor, Grant Holt, class of 2022, about the fact that the magazine was turning 25 in fall of 2021. Bruno had come across an article in the *Kenyon Collegian* where Grant dynamically conceived of creating a 25-year *Persimmons* celebration. After meeting with Grant (remotely, due to the pandemic) Katie and I were so exhilarated that we began immediately collaborating on our memories of Kenyon and *Persimmons*. There was a numinous magic to that serendipitous meeting. Grant seemed to believe, even during this uncertain time, that this celebration was indeed possible; and he thoughtfully offered to orchestrate the event.

We were wonderstruck by his dedication and nourished by the juicy current *Persimmons* magazine, coupled with the knowledge that something we'd sprouted together 25 years ago was not only alive, but thriving. A sudden sense of gratitude to unknown benefactors overtook me. Sort of like how Thich Nhat Hanh described looking at the fruit in your hand while you are eating. When you look deeply, you begin to see all the hands that have been responsible for tending and picking and carrying the fruit to your lips—not to mention the soil, sunlight and water that provided vital sustenance. You feel so much thankfulness arising in you for this gift of fruit, handed to you from strangers and ephemeral elements.

Today, rather serendipitously, one of my current teachers, Chakung Jigme Wangdrak Rinpoche, shared this insight:

> *The fruit that grows on the tree—*
> *we know about the coarse seed, but we can't see*
> *all the subtle stages of development.*
> *So many causes and conditions came together*
> *to create this fruit.*

It set my mind peeling—

How had *Persimmons* grown during this quarter century? How many hands and hearts had helped the magazine remain supple, breathing? What stranger-angel editors had offered their energy toward its fruit seeding from generation to generation? Who would continue to nurture it in future? How many more years would it produce fruit? Another quarter century?

The sense of regeneration and revivification was palpable, tingly. I remember writing in a frenzy at dawn after our meeting, a multitude of correspondences coming to mind. What does it mean to come back to a beloved place of fruition? Another one of my current teachers, Anam Thubten Rinpoche, often teaches how returning to your former visions/versions of selves can feel like returning to previous lifetimes. Disembodied, yet poetically poignant. Revivified, alive, sprouting with clear-sightedness.

Recalling Eavan Boland's visit to Kenyon in November of 1997, for example—her fierce insight, which sings even louder Now that she has crossed over. And Jane Hirshfield's Kenyon reading in 1998, when she disarmed Nostalgia with a cheeky poem. Even still, I well up, overawed by Agha Shahid Ali's radiant generosity when he visited campus in February of 1999, not long before his unforeseen passing. Ever sagacious, his poetry unveils a new resonance Now. While writing *Calling Bell*, many lines from poems and songs we enjoyed at Kenyon wafted up from the churning earth. I greeted them and let them arise, have their say.

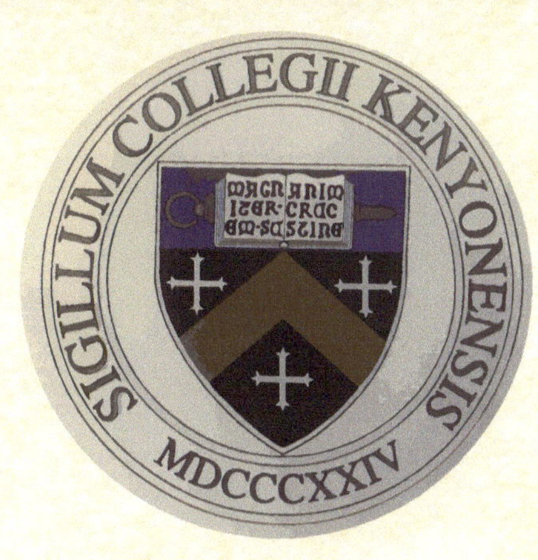

Eavan Boland

with her own words
to distinguish her
from everyone else —

Agha Shahid Ali

One life-changing image that arose in me, from our final year at Kenyon—remember when the monks from Tibet, who trained as artists in exile at the Drepung Loseling Monastery, came and built a Mandala (*dul-tson-kyil-khor*) in the atrium of the Kenyon library, and then we followed them down to the Kokosing River to release the sand to the water? Mounds of rainbow-hued sand consecrated and constructed toward a Radiant Center, over five days— then lovingly at dusk blown into the river and toward the sea—for the sake of healing all sentient beings!

I often think of this image—magnanimous minds, letting this sacred space of careful artwork go—when I think of Kenyon, or *Persimmons*, or anything dearly held. Here I hear Ali incanting: 'Maybe the ages will die away and the loved hands of blessed women will brush the light ashes together?' It is Here, in the Releasing—a love letter on wind carried who knows where— ashes of the beloved scattered free—some kind of eternal vow still abounds.

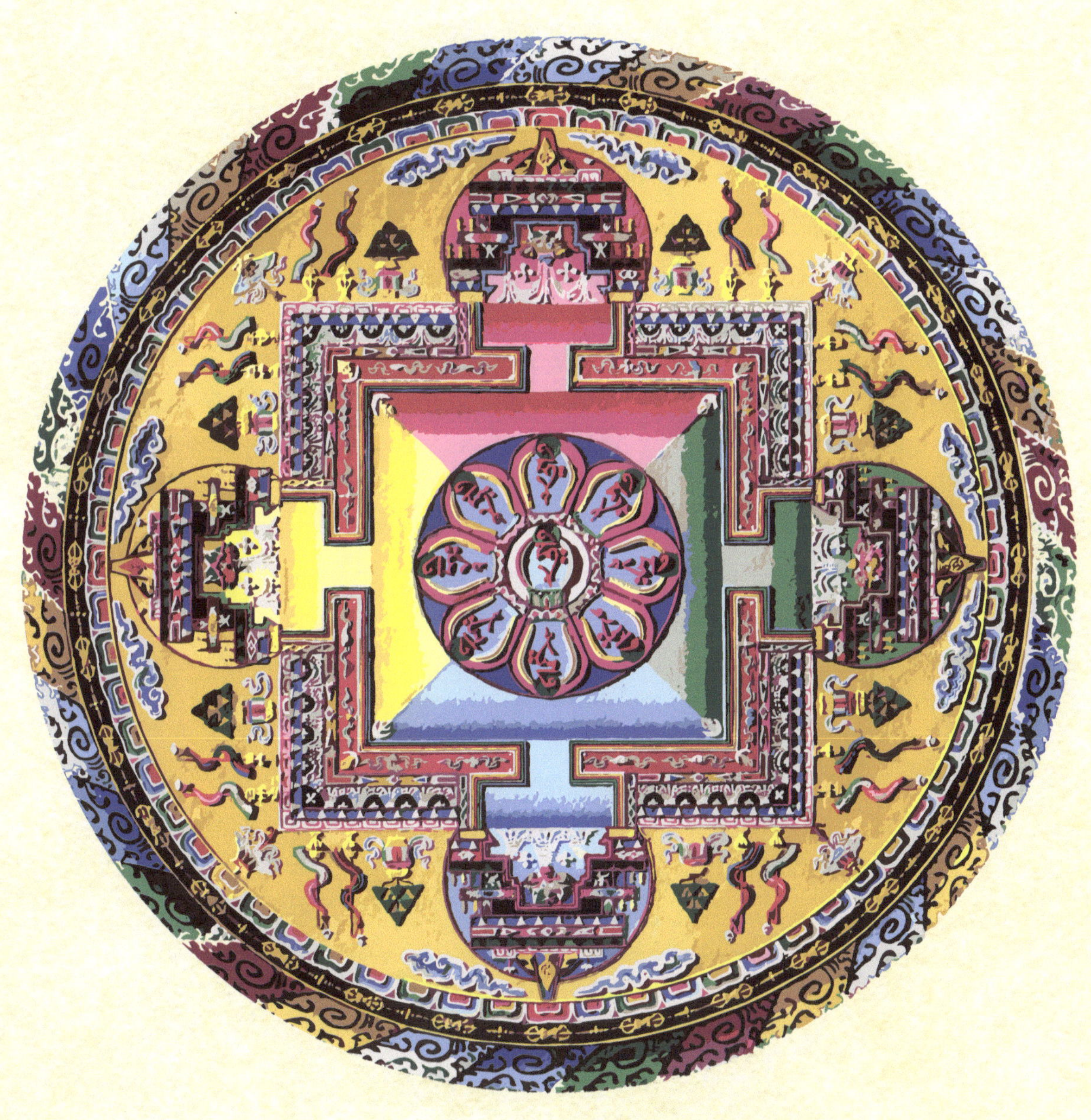

Amitayus Mandala Sand Painting by the Monks of Drepung Loseling Monastery

KP: Somehow time must move differently where you are. You say you wrote 'in a frenzy at dawn'—you sent me your poem speedily. I can't believe you wrote so many pages of beautiful words in such a short time. There was so much to think about and respond to.

I woke up very early that summer morning—it was not so hot that day. The earth seemed to be shouting at us this past summer. Hopefully we will find the best ways to listen. I found quiet dawn time to read your poem five times through. I broke it up into sections so that I could digest it through smaller windows, while also trying to see it as its whole.

I feel like a partner in your poem because so many of the lines of quoted poetry are in my memory too. 'teardrop on fire'—I hadn't noticed the first time I read it; and then the second time, it came to me in song form, and I heard it from memory.

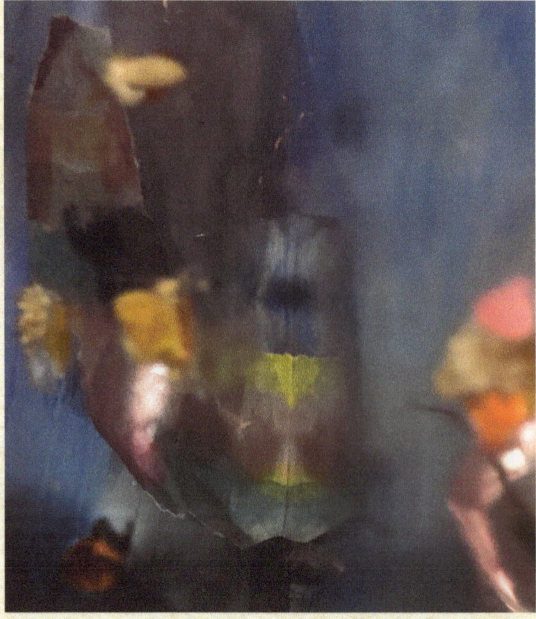

HW: How funny—'Teardrop' was actually a song you shared with me at Kenyon. That song just came up for me out of the ether—while working on our *Calling Bell*, I was also striving feverishly to complete my *Bundling* épopée (a massive poetry project which I started in 2007).

Bundling sprang out of a curious courtship custom from the British Isles, Northern Europe, and colonial North America. Some people who practiced bundling were unable to afford instruments to dance to so they used to sing nonsensical 'mouth music,' or *Puirt à Beul*, which is like making Scottish dance music with your mouth. I learned the song 'Teardrop' by Massive Attack was created and sung by Elizabeth Fraser—the singer from Cocteau Twins, who you also introduced me to at Kenyon. Fraser embodied a new form of mouth music by developing her own ethereal language in which to sing. So when people ask her what her lyrics are or what they mean, she laughs, because it's her own secret language. She says the meaning is located in the sound and the emotion it emits.

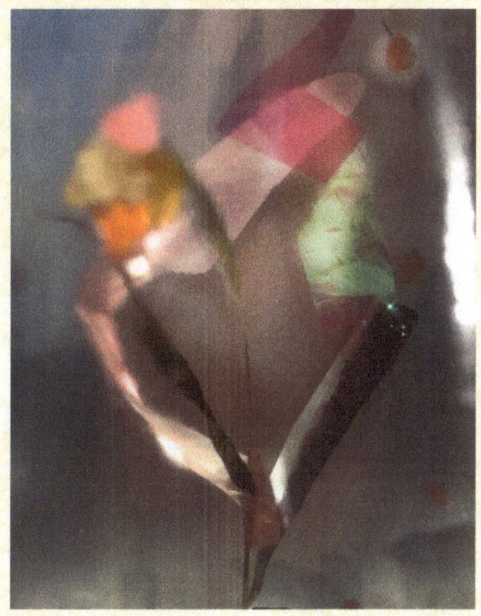

This is actually how I envision my poetry & your art, in conversation with each other—Correspon*dance* of singing-ringing sensory mystery, allowing revelations, inSights, in and through us.

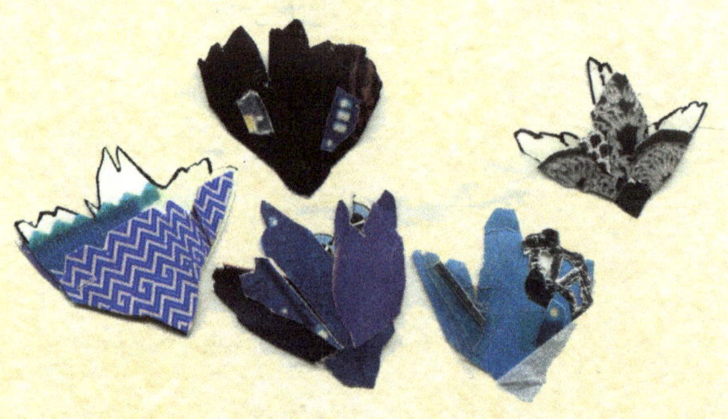

Who knows? Perhaps the same
bird echoed through both of us
yesterday, separate, in the evening—

Recalling now those lines from Rilke, suspended on our freshman room wall. Like 'teardrop on fire'—your chime in my life continues to echo through myriad undulations. The literal lyrics for the song begin: 'Love, love is a verb.' I think so much of our time at Kenyon as a time of active love, of golden light-seeking. Self and World, in dawn, budding, so they could unfurl, unravel, then dissolve. Chasing after a multitudinous Horizon, led around by grasping afflictions, or kleshas, perhaps we didn't know then what we were seeking was already suspiring lumens—Near. Remember how in class Jack Finefrock used to tell us: 'The gold is already gold'? I'm ever learning from that in-spiring koan.

KP: I think your *Calling Bell* poem is about how we learn, and about how we grow toward the light even with obstructions. I don't have a deep understanding of Buddhism, but I have my own path that is probably similar, though has different words; or maybe no words—just paths of light that I follow to find truth. I always think of Professor Rogan's last words to us as we graduated: 'in the future I expect more love and knowledge of you.' I am always asking myself—am I choosing more love and more knowledge; or closing the door and shutting the window?

Now I think about 'Salt Heart' by Jane Hirshfield, that we read at Kenyon so often—

When I read your poem I felt like I was traveling down the path of wisdom or lessons that you gathered at Kenyon and after. The metaphor of river, of body, a middle path, a persimmon and the tree it grows from.   All these things are moving towards what we try to understand as the distance. And how we know distance changes and changes and changes as we move to meet it.

I decided to try to travel down this same path in my own life. Each image relates to something I have learned or am in the process of learning. It is not so much memories but my attempt to try to make visual these points of knowledge. I tried not to think about your poem during this process because I didn't want to try to illustrate the images created by your phrases. I wanted what I was creating to be almost like a traveling companion to your poem. The two would be in conversation across a distance of space and time.

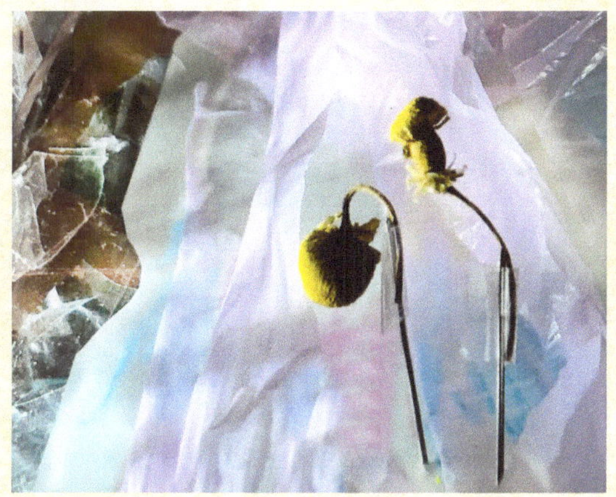

HW: Yes, I remember how you kept returning to the distance. Your vision of that textured landscape, how Kenyon ground for you was made of 'hollows'—I remember your fascination with the word 'lacuna' when we were at Kenyon—how that fertile gap somehow embodied our experience—in the not-yet pregnant Emptiness of 'irrevocable futures' Everything is possible. And how the more we walk along our path, the more our vista seems to amend. As you say, 'distance changes and changes as we move to meet it.' Your 'Flood' piece, which we used for the cover of *Calling Bell*, made me weep—I feel Earth's pang—tender torn fragility—breath being swept up in the deluge. Yet you somehow manage to make the mammoth moment glow with resounding beauty. This art of yours, so resonant for our rip-roaring currents. All-embracing, your generous Eye. When I absorb your luminous art, I behold The Vanishing Point.

KP: When we started our *Calling Bell* project, I'd been thinking about how to face the unknown. I worked on an exhibition with a beautiful artist named Toshiko Takaezu who passed away. I love the way she believed in the unknown and woke up each day awaiting it, like a flower about to blossom in an unknown color.

I want to choose projects that begin with something that I don't understand—a mystery that I may not ever solve but still could come closer to. An unknown thing that I have always thought about was the very particular way that I felt at Kenyon. The place itself felt set apart. When I went to Iceland, I noticed these hollow spaces in the land that seemed to be places where the lava passed over. Maybe they were full of air—I'm not sure— but somehow those little hollows were spared. Kenyon was situated in a hollow. The weather, trees, and moonlight seemed different to me.

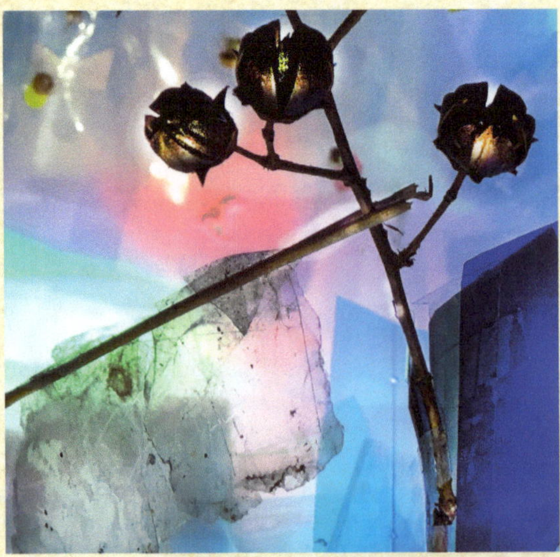

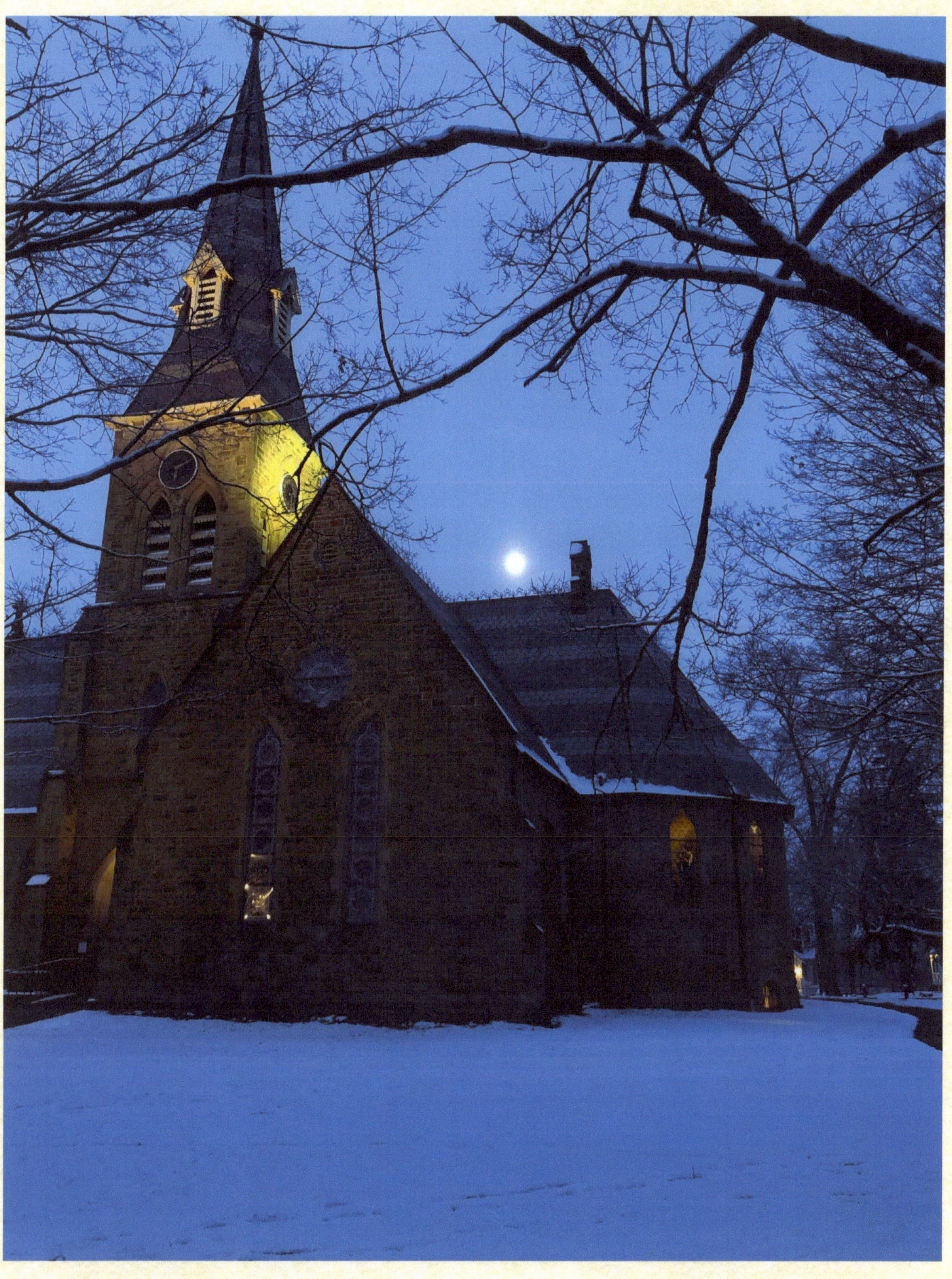

Church of the Holy Spirit in Moonlight, by Grant Holt, Kenyon College, February 2020

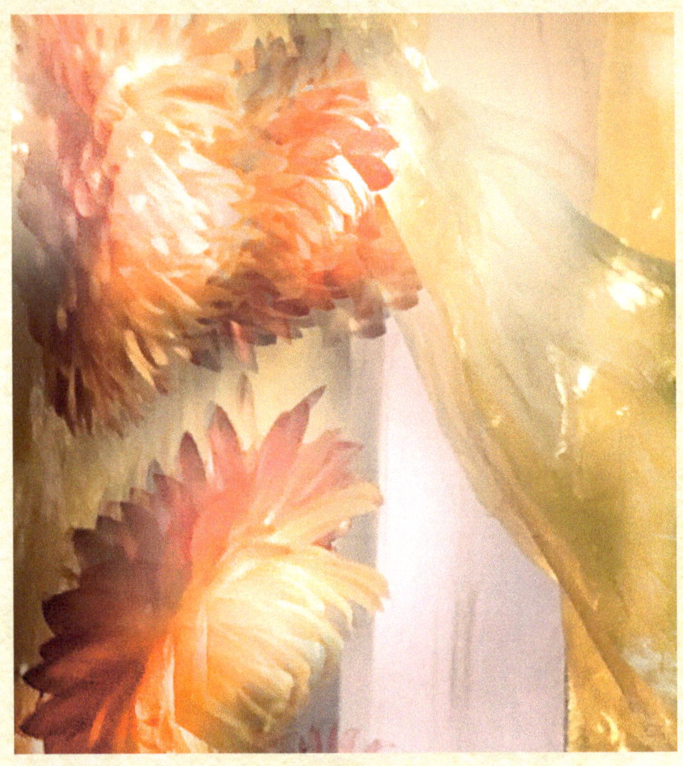

I became so excited about the idea of reaching towards the mystery of the place of Kenyon together. Like we were both standing in a dark hallway, passing one another little pieces of light.

HW: I'd imagined trading light with you in this way since our Kenyon days. Long admired poet-artist collaborations—between Mei-mei Berssenbrugge & Kiki Smith, Barbara Guest & Laurie Reid, Agha Shahid Ali & Izhar Patkin, Erica Hunt & Alison Saar; but I did not see our project shake into being until the *Persimmons* celebration called us to explore a new mystery together.

I noticed while looking again at *Rose*, the book by Li-Young Lee where we found the initial quote for *Persimmons,* that his poem is actually dancing with this very idea—the mystery of creation, memory, the ridges of the ineffable. At the end of the poem, Lee is writing from the perspective of his father, who wore many mythic faces—as a doctor, minister, political prisoner, refugee and artist. His father eventually lost his eyesight but continued painting. In the poem, he is painting persimmons blind, from memory, from Other-realmed senses. From the hollow! That transcend-dance between the word and the image—the Lacuna— where Kenyon resides:

Oh, the feel of the wolftail on the silk,

the strength, the tense

precision in the wrist.

I painted them hundreds of times

eyes closed. These I painted blind.

Some things never leave a person:

scent of the hair of one you love,

the texture of persimmons,

in your palm, the ripe weight.

~Li-Young Lee, 'Persimmons'

About returning to a past abode, Toshiko once said, 'When you come back, it gives another dimension.' Palimpsest of persimmons—layer upon layer of memory, meaning mulled from the vantage point of a fresh mind. Setting foot again inside the hollow, what will we see?

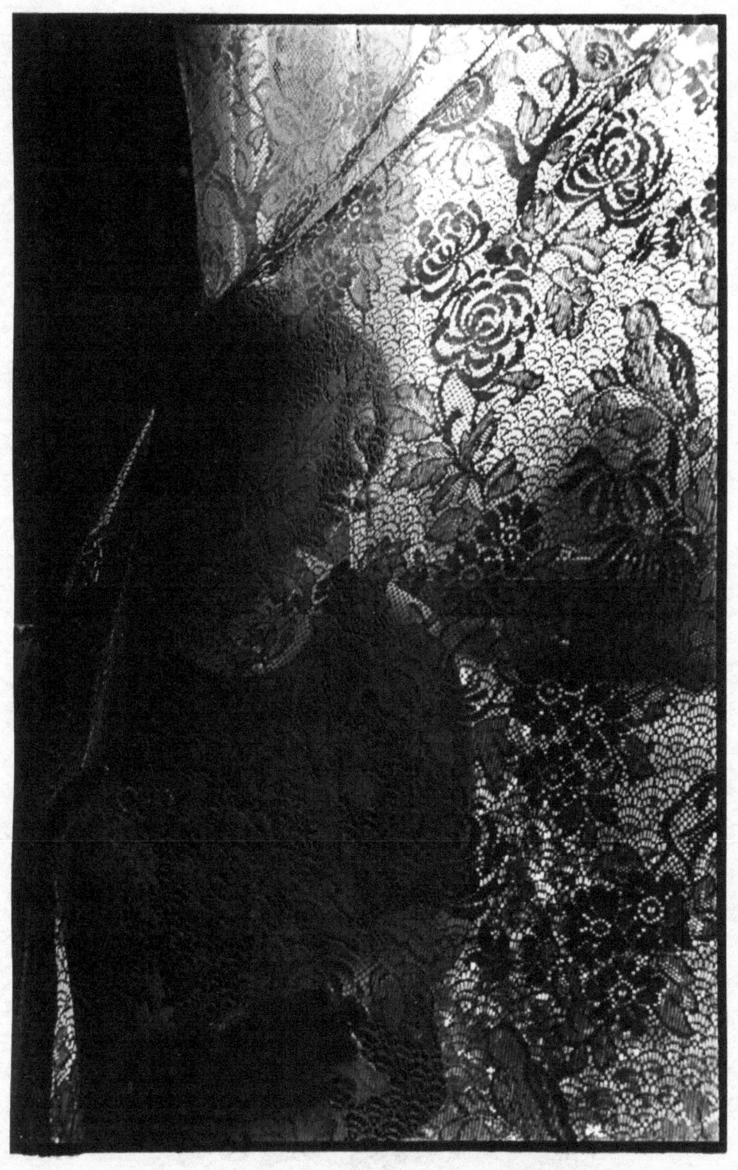

photo by KP of HW, Kenyon College, 1998

in meadows sweet

far from

some

verb

Ophelia

toward world

with

love

Dear Heather,
I have been wanting to make a miniature quilt out of tiny scraps. This is a window quilt with a quilt with a sun rising or setting in its center.

All my love
Karen

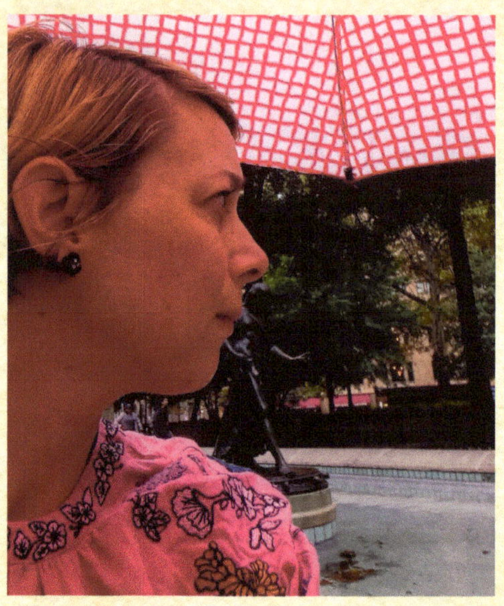

Katie Parry has a MFA from Tyler School of Art and a BA in Studio Art from Kenyon College. She is an artist, mother, and educator living in Philadelphia. She currently works as the Museum Tour Manager at The Fabric Workshop and Museum where she imagines programs, collaborative workshops, and opportunities for exchange.

When Katie remembers Kenyon, she remembers the strange beauty of the trees, the way the moon casts blue shadows, and the kindness of her teachers and friends.

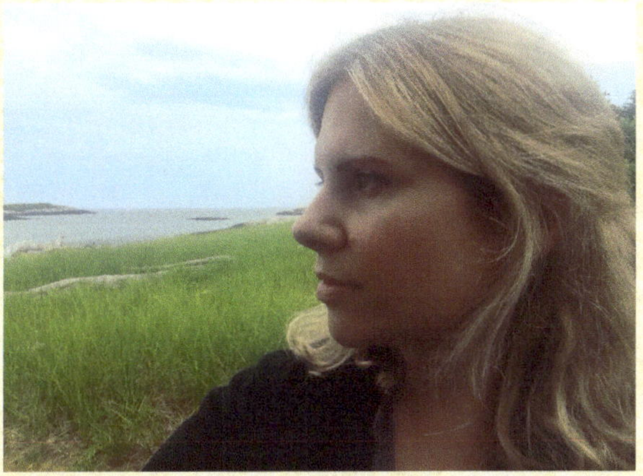

At Kenyon, **Heather Woods** took part in the Synoptic Majors Program and, with the help of luminary mentors, designed her own major concentrating on Comparative Poetics: A study of English, French and Chinese poetry, including translation. During this time, she also served as a Student Associate on the *Kenyon Review*. Returning to her native Bay, Heather received an MFA in Writing from the University of San Francisco and an MFA in Poetry/ Teaching from San Francisco State University.

For the present, Heather and her beloved live along the windswept North Atlantic Coast. By day, she teaches writing to students of all ages; by dawn, she selects and edits books for publication. Her latest épopée, *Bundling*, is forthcoming from Spuyten Duyvil Press in 2022.

When Heather remembers Kenyon days, it is with steadfast, sonorous inspiration:

> *The temple bell stops*
> *But the sound keeps coming*
> *Out of the flowers*

> ~ Bashō

Acknowledgments

Both the Author and the Artist are grateful to Grant Holt, and the current *Persimmons* staff, for their vital vision in bringing this celebration to fruition; Kenyon College, for generously supporting the journey; and the *Kenyon Review*, for kindly hosting the hybrid event.

Ever grateful to our fellow *Persimmons* editors, for offering their tireless energy, skillful minds, and boundless passion to ensuring enduring voices seed:

Courtney Bambrick, Alissa Clark, Alyssa Croft, Chris Cook, Monica Cure, Nathan Gardner, Lisa Groesz, Caitlin Horrocks, Lindsey Maurer, Zach Nowak, Addie Palin, Kirsten Reiners, Clara Rubin-Smith, Jesse Savage, Amy Shapiro, Jascha Smilack, Rachel Soleta, Bruno Trindade, Ben Vore, Katie Wallace, Molly Warren

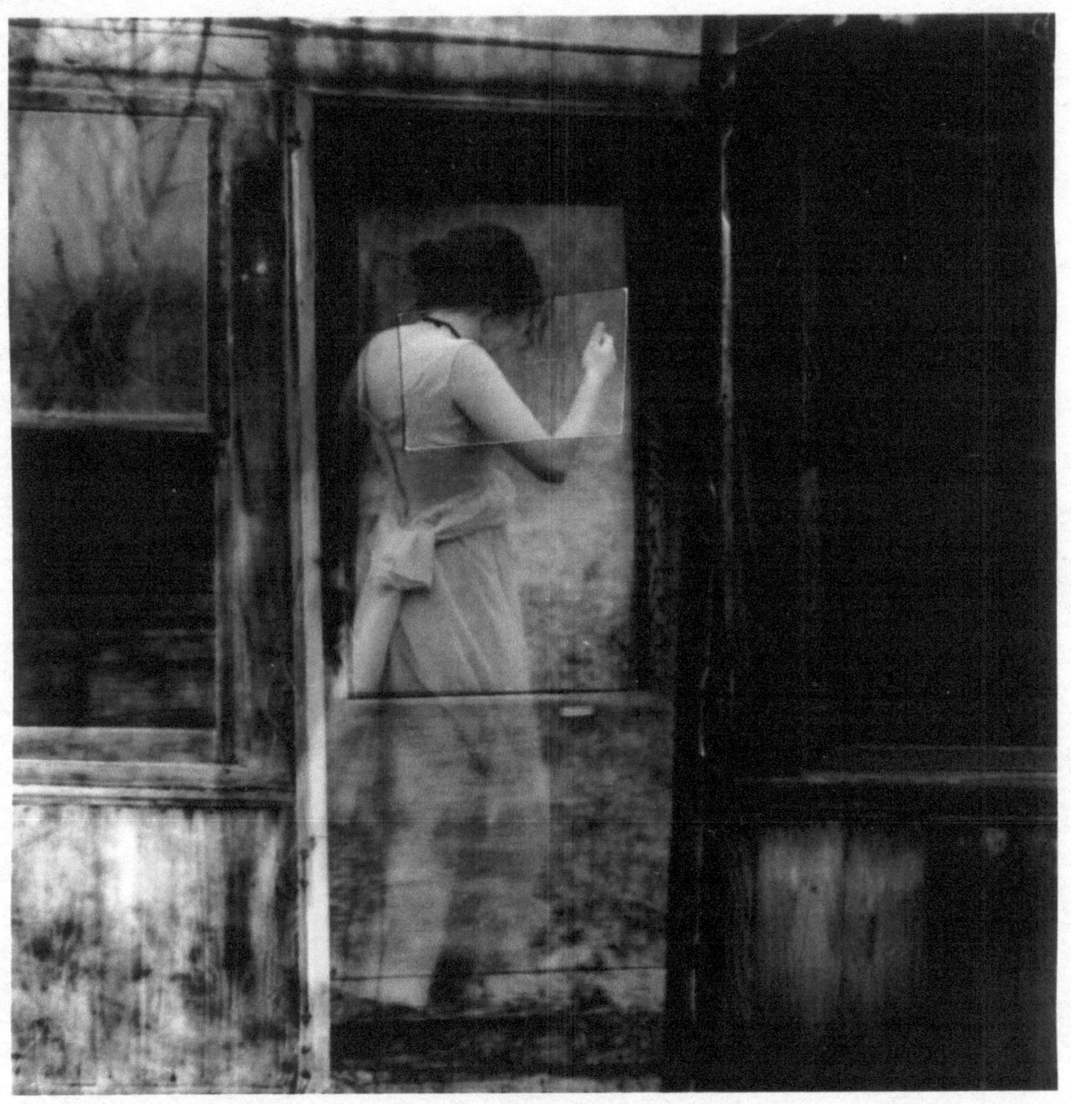

"Face In Transition" by Emily Harris. *Persimmons*, Spring 1997

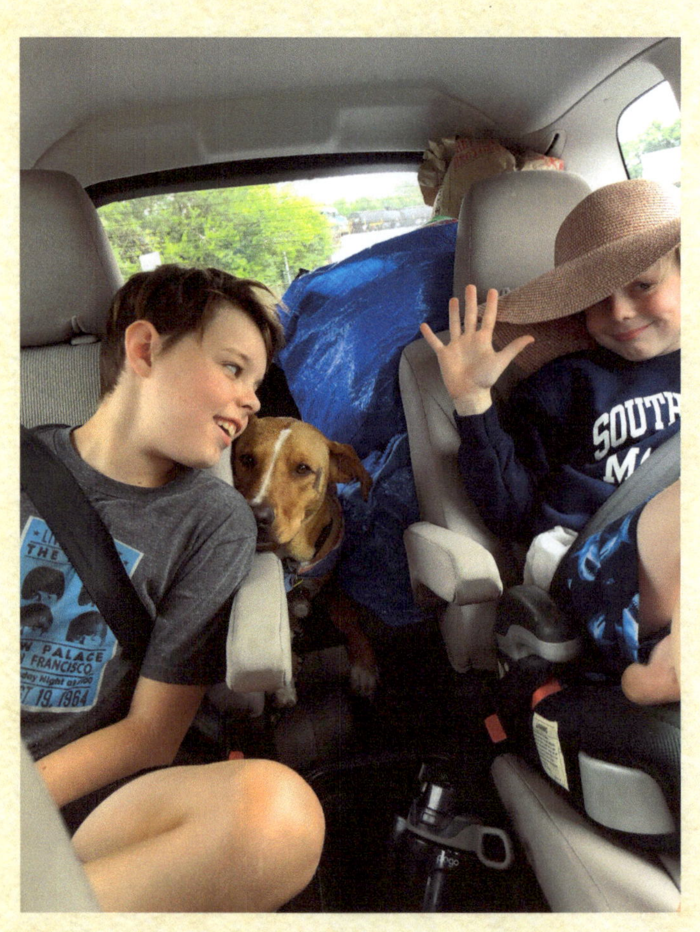

KP:

Thank you to Martin Garhart, for teaching us how to draw with a tenderness for all that we see.

Thank you, Claudia Esslinger, for lighting a fire in me and for the rare opportunity to swim in an 80's power suit down the Kokosing river.

Thank you to Jack Finefrock, for allowing me to go wildly off course when translating Chinese poetry and for asking me to turn the diseased tree branches in his yard into shrines.

Thank you to Lewis Hyde for helping me understand the very particular way that I could be an artist in the world.

Thank you—Mom, Dad, and my sister Meghan, for all their love and for trusting me to follow my own way. Thank you to my husband Thom, my sons Dai and Cove, and our dog Kleo, for making my life so full.

HW:

Thank you to my Kenyon professors, especially Jianhua Bai, Jean Blacker, Jennifer Clarvoe, Jack Finefrock, Mort Guiney, James Kimbrell, Ted Mason, and Kim McMullen for inspiring, inquiring, and enlightening my mind-heart wide.

Thank you to the *Kenyon Review*, for helping me dive into the depths of reel-world publishing.

Thank you to Alissa (Clark) Bell, Emily Harris, Katie (Wallace) Karys, and Laura Vazquez for embodying loving Kenyon kindness.

Thank you to Kenyon, for integrating Tagore's truth: "The highest education is that which does not merely give us information but makes our life in harmony with all existence."

Thank you to my very Californian parents, for offering my studies a chance to flower in secluded pastoral verdancy.

Eternal thanks and longevity to my current Sangha, the Dharma bearers—Dharmata Foundation, Abhaya Fellowship and Sravasti Abbey.

Much merit to mon mari, for walking the Noble Path with me.

All merit is shared; all mistakes are my own.

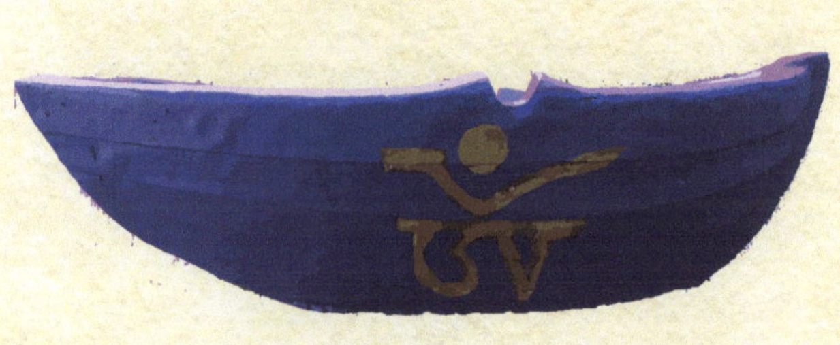

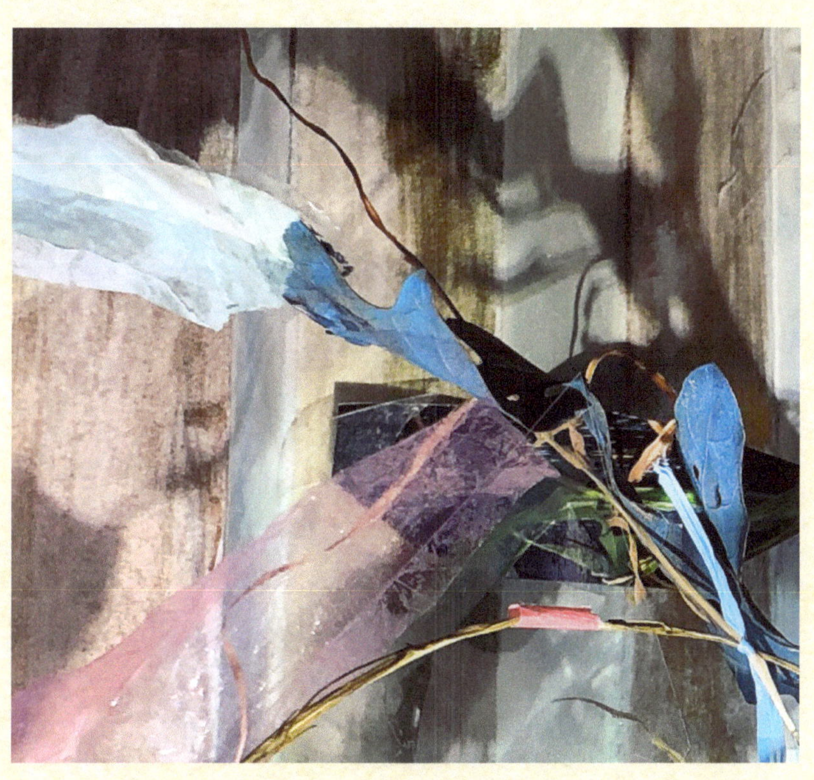

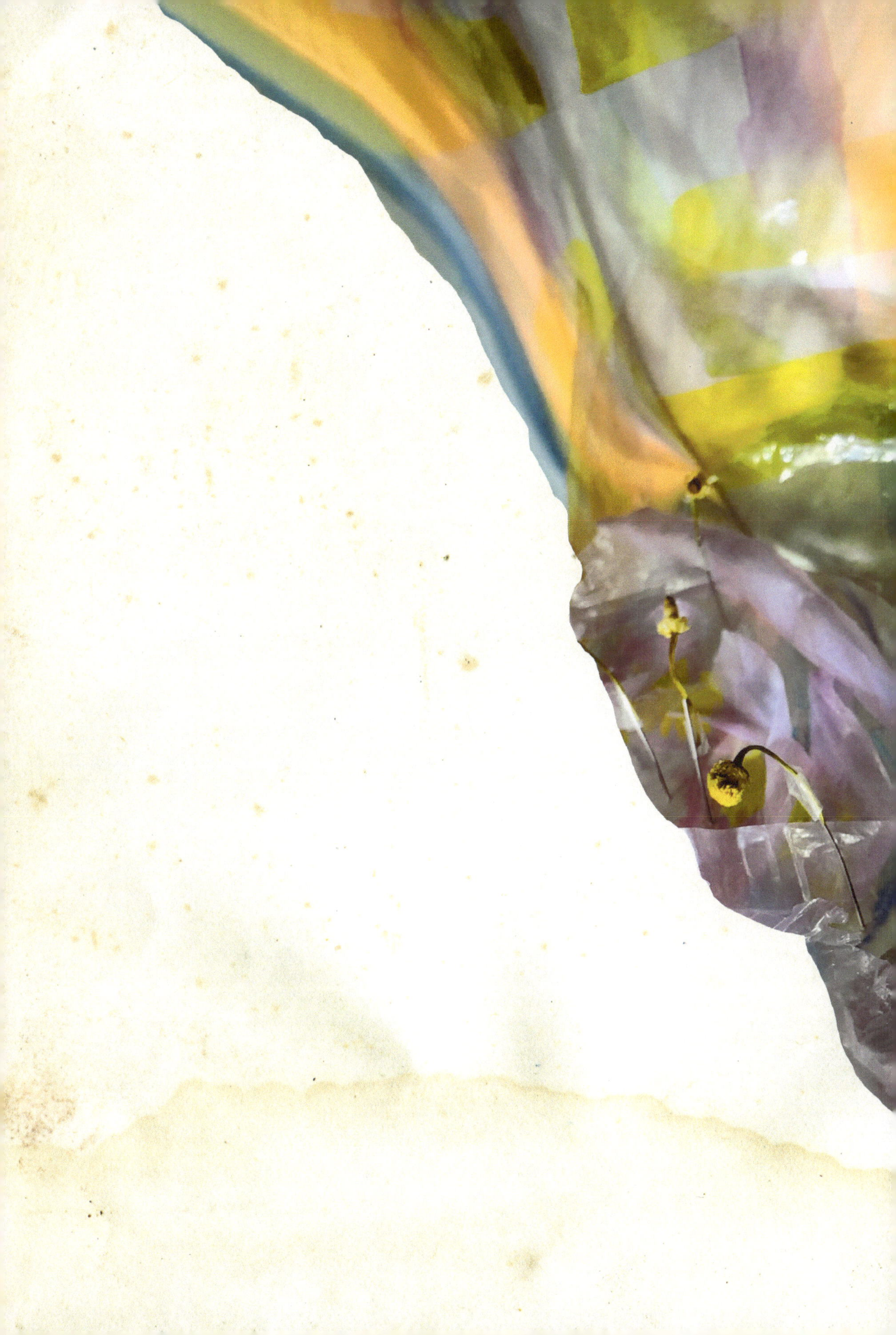

www.ingramcontent.com/pod-product-compliance
Lightning Source LLC
Chambersburg PA
CBHW042150030726
47599CB00004B/682